A *Bipolar* GOSPEL

A New Voyage through the
Gospel from the Perspective of
a Bipolar II Survivor

Henry Williams

LUMINARE PRESS
WWW.LUMINAREPRESS.COM

A BIPOLAR GOSPEL
A New Voyage through the Gospel from the
Perspective of a Bipolar II Survivor
© 2018 Henry Williams

"Here Between: A Poem Trio" © 2018 by Bryn Phinney.
Printed by permission of the author.

"From a Theme on Julian's Chapter XX" © 1987 by Denise Levertov.
Reprinted by permission of New Directions Publishing Corporation.

Scripture quotations are from the New Revised Standard Version Bible,
copyright © 1989 National Council of the Churches of Christ in the
United States of America. Used by permission. All rights reserved.

Wisdom quotation is from the New Revised Standard Version Bible:
Catholic Edition, copyright © 1989, 1993 National Council of the
Churches of Christ in the United States of America. Used by permission.
All rights reserved.

Printed in the United States of America

Cover Design: Melissa Lund
Luminare Press
438 Charnelton St., Suite 101
Eugene, OR 97401
www.luminarepress.com

LCCN: 2018950763
ISBN: 978-1-944733-94-0

To Shari and Craig Buma

Who housed my mother and me after I left the hospital

TABLE OF CONTENTS

Preface

This book is a retelling of the Christian story as seen through the lens of my experience with bipolar II disorder. Bipolar II is characterized by both depression and hypomania, which is a less intense form of the mania which people living with bipolar I experience. While I hope that my experiences will resonate with those who know bipolar disorder intimately, I do not intend to speak on behalf of every Christian who suffers it. This is why this book is called A *Bipolar Gospel*: it is a single offering from one member of the great cloud of witnesses to Christ.

All my knowledge of psychology comes from therapy, amateur research, and conversation. My lack of expertise in the field of psychology may frustrate those who seek anything more than a first-hand account of symptoms and casually academic reflections on them. For more information on mental illness, please visit the website of the National Alliance on Mental Illness, nami.org.

If you or a loved one is in danger of suicide, call a medical professional or the national suicide hotline: 1-800-273-8255.

Thanks to Dave Sikkenga for inviting me to share early reflections on my experience in the hospital for the Sunday school of Wheaton Christian Reformed Church. Thanks to Dr. Jill Baumgaertner for her generous encouragements as I embarked on the daunting task of writing this book. Thanks also to Vern Geurkink, who allowed me to bounce excited ideas off him over English muffins at his retirement home.

Thanks to the 71 backers who funded this book on Kickstarter or otherwise, especially Tasha and James Bartholomew, Drake Williams Jr., Kathy Tsen, Elise Bock, Shari and Craig Buma, Josh Doty, Daniel McHenney, Dustin Northcutt, Kirsten and Dave Forshew, Kyle and Wendy Haack, Sam Beatrice, and Lisa Ohlen Harris.

Thanks to Dan and Mary Sytsma, who housed me while I was writing this book.

Thanks to those who took care of me when I could not keep myself safe, especially Joe Tam, Dustin Northcutt, Katherine Harrison, Elizabeth Bretscher, Janelle Buford, Susan Anderson, Kyle Haack, Stephen Read, Brady Woods, Kristen Niemitalo, Craig and Shari Buma, Drake, Andrea, Abigail, and Samuel Williams, and Laurie Harris.

Thanks finally to my parents, Drake and Andrea Williams, who proofread the manuscript. Thanks to my mother-in-law, Lisa Ohlen Harris, who also proofread and walked me through the process of publishing. Thanks also to Todd and Lisa Harris for housing Laurie and me when both of us were unable to work because of my illness. And thanks especially to my wife Laurie Harris, whose unfailing care and encouragement are the bedrock of my life.

Foreword

In our modern world, "quick tips" and "easy steps" to support your mental health are available at every turn. This sometimes gives the impression that emotional wellness should be easy. If you can just follow a few quick and easy steps—exercise more regularly, connect with caring friends, think more positively, etc.—you will be emotionally stable and feel happy every day. This is the new face of stigma concerning mental health, a redesigned method of saying "just get over it."

In reality, mental wellness is hard. The "tips and steps" are generally not untrue, but for many of us, they are neither quick nor easy in the midst of human suffering. This is especially the case for those of us who have been diagnosed with mental illness. Exercising regularly can feel like the equivalent of carrying a huge bag of bricks around in the midst of a major depressive episode. The availability of close connections can seem impossibly elusive in the grips of social anxiety. And thinking positively is the hardest thing in the world in the confusing jumble of a thought disorder.

Christ offers a different path, a deeper and more authentic response to suffering that is neither quick nor easy: the way of the cross. This most universal symbol of Christianity reminds us that God knows and shares our suffering. Interestingly enough, God does not eliminate suffering in our human experience—there are few things more sure than the reality of suffering in some shape and form for every person on earth. But God has given us everything we need to endure and even grow through our suffering.

The way of the cross is a path that does not allow us to ignore, eliminate, or deny our suffering. There are no quick fixes on the way of the cross. This path requires us to acknowledge when we hurt, to lean into our pain, even to embrace our challenges. It requires us to open up to our experience of suffering in order to learn all there is to learn along the way. And in one of the greatest mysteries of God's creative power, this opening up to our suffering is what leads us repeatedly back to joy.

There is much overlap here with the world of evidence-based psychology. Moving out of pain avoidance and into curious observation of our experience is the foundation of many therapeutic models. As a clinical psychologist, I can say that many a healing transformation has emerged out of that moment in the therapy room when a client says or does the thing of which they are most afraid. We might be afraid of the dark, but God is not.

In light of this reality, the Christian church has much to offer when it comes to mental wellness. From the beginning of Christ's ministry on earth, he modeled authentic and broken community—community that welcomed (even sought) the broken and hurting. His harshest words were reserved for those who feigned perfection. His warmest welcome was reserved for those who knew their brokenness. And in many places, the Christian church continues to be a community that allows for authentic brokenness. Within true Christian community, there is opportunity to acknowledge our hurt, to lean together into our pain, and even to embrace our challenges together. There is opportunity to walk the way of the cross communally, to journey the difficult path of endurance and growth as a family of faith. There is opportunity to practice deep, authentic responses to mental pain that help us grow and open up pathways to joy.

In this book, you will find one such example of an authentic Christian walk. With openness, truthfulness, and hard-won wisdom, Williams provides us a window into his journey through the illness of bipolar II as a young adult. He also shares his philosophical insights into the Christian gospel as seen through this vulnerable journey of suffering. The result is an inspiration for all of us to walk the way of the cross as we encounter suffering, to openly acknowledge our pain (and the pain of others) so that we can be available for God's deep, patient, enduring work in our lives. It is a call to growth, an encouragement to be open in the midst of challenge so that God's light can shine through the cracks of our brokenness.

> ...*we boast in our hope of sharing the glory of God. And not only that, but we also boast in our sufferings, knowing that suffering produces endurance, and endurance produces character, and character produces hope, and hope does not disappoint us, because God's love has been poured into our hearts through the Holy Spirit that has been given to us.*
>
> *Romans 5:2b–5*

Irene Kraegel, PsyD

Director, Center for Counseling and Wellness,
Calvin College
www.themindfulchristian.net

Introduction

I grew up as a missionary kid in the Netherlands. Every couple of years, my family and I would travel to Austria for our mission organization's conference. As we gathered each morning to sing, pray, and listen to scripture, we would hear a sermon by the international director of the organization, evangelist Vincent Price. Vincent is renowned for his ageless zeal for the gospel cause. He would tell us of how he shared the word with countless masses in a stadium in Latvia (or wherever it was), and of the thousands who came to the makeshift altar that night to receive Christ. His message was simple: even though all of humanity has strayed from God's commands, Jesus died on the cross on your behalf so that you could be made right with God today. Just pray to accept him into your heart as Savior and Lord, and though the world may despise you, heaven is yours.

I look around the room with my mind's eye. Two booths down is Pishta, a fifty-something who runs an orphanage in Hungary and drives a communist-era van with empty Coke bottles and bowling ball-sized rocks rolling around on its floor. Across the room is Pedro, my Spanish friend, who speaks in broken English and plays pool with me in the basement, our cupped hands poised to rescue the balls from the caverns of the pool table and save ourselves the euro charge for a new game. On the other side of the room are the Ukrainian Baptists, a zealous group who speak of God's work in the courage of Ukrainian nationalists who peacefully resisted the Russian invasion of Crimea. Just to the left is the Slovakian fellow who, when I mentioned my desire to pursue a degree in philosophy, offered me warnings on the dangers of secular thought from his latest book on the subject. On the right with the guitars is the multigenerational Romanian contingent, easily the most cheerful group in the crowd.

These people could hardly understand each other. Many of them were poorly educated, and I can only imagine how much of a strain the week's retreat was on their budgets. They were career missionaries, which means that, in a sense, they had no careers. They had given their lives to God as modern zealots for his word. Their single treasure was the knowledge that they had been saved by God and were sent by him to a dying continent to do the most meaningful of work—saving souls.

For all these reasons, I had an increasingly difficult time relating to them as I grew older.

Even so, I caught the missionary impulse. In high school I kept a stash of free Bibles in my locker and gave them out to any schoolmates who showed the faintest interest in Christianity. I learned some apologetic arguments and eagerly tried them out on those of my friends who were admitted atheists. The results were less than satisfying: I wasn't able to convince them of the intellectual self-evidence of the faith. Sensitive to the call "to be a witness," I made friends for the sake of proselytizing them, and even gained a convert somehow. In my last years of high school, I spent an hour or more each day praying and reading scripture. Just like those stalwart missionaries, I believed firmly that the gospel was the most important thing in the world, so I prayed tirelessly that it would be spread in my secular high school. I worked diligently, overcame difficulties with French and math, and graduated with the title of "Most Outstanding Student" for my efforts with the school's student-run charity organization. In the eyes of my family, I was a roaring success.

But underneath the Christian self I had constructed lay an interior darkness that became harder and harder to ignore. It first showed its head in my response to my classmates' bullying. While being teased relentlessly for dancing with an autistic girl at a fifth grade dance, I quickly learned to stifle my emotions of sadness and anger and replace them with angst and a nervous laughter. To mask my shame, I grew resentful and vindictive. While I had always assumed that my faith in God set me apart from my classmates, almost all of whom were uninterested in religion, there was little in my thought or behavior as a young adult to suggest that I served a God of love. From this emotional poverty arose a nagging and sometimes devastating doubt.

During a feverish month of disbelief, I examined the evidence for and against Jesus' resurrection for hours upon hours. In the throes of wasting skepticism, I determined that if I discovered that the resurrection was improbable I would kill myself. Mercifully, I survived that month, believing firmly that Christ did indeed rise from the dead.

Even so, my doubts would recur throughout the rest of high school and into college. I now see clearly that my foibles were not primarily academic or theoretical. What I ultimately yearned for was not assurance that the faith that I held was self-evident, but an authentic way of relating to God and to other people. I longed for a God who saw me and loved me throughout my teenage angsts, and I thirsted for the confidence needed to hold the gaze of another and speak earnestly and charitably.

Hydra-like, the darkness from which my resentfulness and doubt arose also produced a crippling anxiety. For the months surrounding my sixteenth birthday, I lived in constant fear of vomiting. The fear was precipitated by a minor stomach flu and long outlived it, taking me out of school for days on end, postponing my birthday party, and making life miserable. I assumed that my troubles were simply proportionate to my lot as a Christian high schooler at an antagonistically secular school. My subtle self-righteousness, solidified in the well-intentioned belief that I was to somehow bring God to my high school, also cloaked the extent to which my own life was in desperate need of repair. I graduated from high school with the illusions of my own success and stability still intact, and brought them to Wheaton College, an elite evangelical school near Chicago.

In hindsight, it seems implausible that my complex of insecurities, resentment, and misgivings might have gradually dissipated in a Christian environment. But that is what I believed upon matriculation, even though I didn't call my specters by name. For a time, this assumption went relatively unchallenged. Anxieties surrounding friends and work during my freshman year were chalked up to the adjustment of being at school; the lifelessness and spiritual exhaustion of my sophomore year was explained by the supposedly endemic Wheaton "sophomore slump." At Wheaton College, the sophomore slump is understood to be primarily a spiritual phenomenon and the term is invoked to explain one's lack of Christian zeal. But my internal darkness rapidly grew beyond the bounds of a sophomore slump and became too large, too wild to ignore. At the end of sophomore year, I underwent a month in which I was almost entirely out of touch with my emotions; when someone asked me how I was doing, I replied in earnest, "I don't actually know."

By the same time junior year, I was in shambles because I had been rejected by a woman whom I thought God had told me I was going to marry. While I had devoutly prayed about the matter for over a year, God seemed to have forgotten to give her the memo. As I came to grips with the unreliability of what I had perceived to be God's voice, I strayed closer to suicide than ever before. Fortunately, I was able to rely on the strength of some incredibly caring and gracious friends to make it through the darkness—and the remainder of the semester. I no longer believed that God was exactly who I imagined him to be. Sitting in the ruins of my broken beliefs about God, I finally began to take his transcendence seriously. Now I knew—studying at a Christian college could not defend me from the darkness within.

Fall: traditionally a time of beauty. In September of my senior year, I had just started a new relationship. I should have been happy. But something was odd. For the last two years, the beginning of fall had been a glad hiatus to my winter and springtime depressions. But this time I felt burdened, as if in the last moment before running a race I had been given a five-pound pack: just enough to be irksome; not enough to be debilitating. I remember stopping in front of the door of my apartment after a long day at school and wondering why the season that had long been so kind to me was now proving so burdensome. During this time I was given to vertiginous mood swings from near-ecstasy to anxiety to lifelessness within a matter of hours. As the semester progressed, my anxiety at my ever more precarious mental state increased. Friendships bent under the pressure and the relationship begun at the end of the summer did not survive November.

Thanksgiving: traditionally a time of joy and gratitude. As I sat with my family around the table, life seemed almost normal—for all of fifteen minutes. The rest of the weekend was simply bleak. In a cruel twist of fate, the depression I found myself in both caused and was caused by the misery my ex-girlfriend and I had just suffered. Now the hours of relative well-being became rare; darkness was to become my new normal.

From my personal journal in early January:

> Well-being is now measured on an entirely different scale—"well" stands for a glimmer of hope which lasts long enough to be credible, "decent" for when I'm not an immediate danger to self or others, and "poorly" for when the earth has tipped off its axis entirely. I almost feel sorry for those who kindly ask me how I am doing, if they really want to know, because I cannot truly tell them without radically changing our relationship and the mood of the conversation. And those I can tell...I am fearful of scaring them off.

Winter: traditionally a time of death, cold, and darkness. Hours and hours of numbing pain, no end in sight. I tried and tried, but I could not stop myself from being depressed. This in turn led to obsessive thoughts, which led to more depression. During my first weeks of antidepressants, I experienced four-day long hypomanic spikes: bursts of joy, energy, and productivity that seemed to come out of nowhere. But these spikes were short-lived, followed ever more predictably by days more in my inner dungeon. From this dungeon, I tried hard to communicate my situation with those around me. Since I still appeared more or less normal, many had a hard time believing that I was depressed, and few but my therapist and closest friends could imagine the desolation that was to come.

I withdrew further into myself. Reading is often a depressing activity for me, but when I had nothing to do, I often foolishly tried to take refuge in a book instead of seeking a more immediate, reciprocal companionship. Thoughts of self-harm, which at the first had only been occasional radar-blips, became commonplace. I have repeated memories of climbing the outdoor stairs to my college apartment, hearing the iconic Union Pacific freight trains hauling down the rails a football field away...and shuddering. Johnny Cash's song about adultery and execution, "Long Black Veil," looped and looped in my mind as I sought catharsis from the oppressive weight of darkness within. Even as I began psychiatric treatment, my mind semi-consciously began to assume that I would soon die. I left an interview for the summer job I would later take wondering if I would even survive the semester.

There were plenty of other indications that my state was on a dangerous trajectory indeed. My sleeping and eating patterns were irregular, my relationships with all but my closest friends uncomfortable, and my few treasured friendships strained by the weight of depression. Upon returning from an otherwise marvelous Christmas break with family in South Africa, I made a point of not mentioning the trip to friends, because then I would have to explain why I enjoyed it so little. I started to worry about whether I would compulsively hurt those around me, and sometimes spent entire conversations petrified by the thought that I would harm the person I was talking to. I began group therapy for social anxiety, which was clearly the wrong group for me, since by then I was caught in the tumult of bipolar depression and generalized, obsessive anxiety. My illness had become so powerful that the weekly group, the personal therapy, and the medication I was taking could do little to cure it.

Spring: traditionally a time of hope and new birth. Also the time of Lent. As the Christians I knew prepared their hearts for prayer, my Lenten gloom was simply a continuation and a fleshing out of the depression that preceded and transcended it. From my journal on Ash Wednesday:

> Was more depressed today than any time since January—ouch. 5 mg of Lex[apro] is not working. Most of today was spent fasting and being depressed, and most of being depressed was spent fighting off thoughts of destruction. God, when will I figure this thing out? When will I stop being so miserably depressed and when will not causing disaster stop being such an effort?

I grew increasingly frustrated at my condition, and self-accusation had long before become an hourly routine. While the flowers burst forth in color, externalizing and realizing the inner beauty that had long been inarticulate within them, I vacuum-sealed my spirit, internalized the profound anger I was feeling, and turned it against myself. My ability to contain my rabid depression was evaporating, and thoughts of externalizing it in suicide grew ever more pressing.

And then? Near-despair, a week in the behavioral health ward, back to school, through intensive therapy, and eventually to an uncertain equilibrium, the stability of motion. Motion toward faith, toward hope, toward love, toward God, I hope. The rest of this book is about my journey through the hospital and my story since then. But it's about much more than that, too. Though I cringe at the thought of being an evangelist and though finding common cause with those many European missionaries that I grew up with seems near impossible, this book is, despite itself, evangelism pure and simple: a retelling of the Christian gospel. I find myself presenting the gospel in such a way that its contents are in constant conversation with my own experience of the presence—and the absence—of God through my experience with mental illness. I tell it for the sake of everyone I've talked to while writing this book, who almost without exception knows someone with mental illness, is involved in treating it, or suffers it themself. I tell it because the gospel, in all the forms that it has taken throughout the millennia, begs to be shared. It is not as though we start with the task of saving souls and turn to the words of scripture as a tool in that task; rather, we tell the Christian story because it is *worth telling*. And I tell it more than anything else for the sake of the mentally ill within the church, who are so often told to cram their suffering within the pious platitudes offered to them by those who are not willing to reckon with the paradoxes of suffering. If just one reader finds a shadow of the gospel in this book, then these many hours of writing will all have been worth it.

Chaos

A wind from God swept over the face of the waters.[1]

H ere is one of the relatively few things that I've learned while fighting mental illness over the last decade: if I don't know what I'm feeling, what I'm feeling is probably nothing good. Many people imagine that depression is simply a besetting sadness that will not lift. While consistent sadness is indeed a hallmark of depression, sadness is only one of a range of symptoms that can occur in a depressed mind. Another one: numbness.

Physical numbness means that the body has lost sensation in one of its members. Emotional numbness means that the heart has lost sensation partially or altogether. Physical numbness generally comes with the knowledge that part of one's body is unfeeling. Emotional numbness oftentimes comes with no such warning. In fact, one's mind can continue for weeks, even months, at a time before recognizing that it is unreceptive.

At the end of my sophomore year of college, I was almost entirely alienated from my own emotions. The prayer, fasting, and scripture reading I had practiced so

---

1   Genesis 1:2

diligently that year had taught me not to be attentive to my interior state, but rather to ignore it—a chronic tendency I have while attempting to commune with God. As friend after friend asked me how I was, I earnestly replied "I don't know," or, in my less vulnerable moments, "OK." To be truthful, I didn't really want to know what I was experiencing. Months of spiritual and emotional frustration had left me in a miserable state. I tried harder to pray, but found no release. I didn't think my emotions were important at all and tried to avoid them. Several times that year, I had been near overcome with desire for a romantic relationship but found only rejection and dismay. The result: fear, anger, sadness, guilt, shame, disgust. The fact that I was not perceiving these emotions did nothing to change their inchoate dominion over me; in fact, their hiddenness gave them strength. I felt these emotions and trembled at their power over me, but consciously I could not even name them. Since I could not name them, I could not control them. Since I could not control them, they began to control me, working both chaos and its thick concealment within the depths of my soul.

Several people I know are convinced that the theory of macroevolution is unbiblical and should be rejected on theological grounds. I know even more who are convinced that the Darwinist model of evolution poses no particular threat to the historic Christian affirmation of the creation of everything by God *ex nihilo*. But relatively few Christians from the circles I grew up in are interested in reading the creation account found in Genesis as an epic, which is disheartening. Since the creation account is not a scientific account of how various objects came into being, it should not be read primarily in relation to such scientific accounts, but rather within the genre in which it was written, which is ancient creation epic. In short, the reader of Genesis 1 and 2 should pay much more attention to the Babylonian creation myth *Enuma Elish* than *On the Origin of Species* because Genesis was written within the literary context of the former, not the latter. One of the aspects that distinguishes the Genesis account among ancient creation epics is the utter sovereignty of God over all created matter, including all other spiritual forces.

But curiously, although the Genesis account never posits multiple dueling deities as other ancient Near Eastern accounts do, it still mentions a primordial chaos: "and the Spirit of God hovered over the face of the waters."[2] For the ancient Israelites, water symbolized anything unruly, unpredictable, and dangerous. After all, they lived on the shores of the great Mediterranean, the sea that would daunt their oppressors, the mighty Romans, over a millennium after Israel settled Canaan. The waters in the context of the Genesis account are primarily metaphorical and thus symbolize a state of chaos pre-existing God's sovereign ordering of the world. And I wonder about that chaos, because at times my very soul seems to be made of its stuff. So often, the emotional monsoons that characterize my inner life seem to have been brought from the primordial chaos to the present as a remnant of pre-creation bedlam.

When chaos replaces order, the result is nothingness. I am most harmful to myself and to others if I do not know what emotions I am experiencing. Subconscious fear makes me defensive and bossy, subconscious shame renders me indecisive and withdrawn, subconscious anger exhausts me.

---

2   Genesis 1:2

But where there is chaos, God creates and calls us to create. The act of naming is essential to creation, because to "call each thing by its right name"[3] is both to capture what it already is and to determine what it shall be. One of my particular tasks as someone prone to internal chaos is to create meaning from it precisely by naming its elements. When I can identify and communicate that I'm feeling anxious or joyful or despondent, I enter into deeper communion with others. Furthermore, we don't need to identify our feelings on our own. It is cathartic for me when someone says "it sounds like you're really guilty about this," or "wow, you're happy today!" We have no indication that the creative act of naming was completed in the Genesis account; if anything, it started in earnest when humans were given the task of naming the animals under their care. This naming perpetuated the word of God that gave the earth its being and extended it in the richness of creaturely identity and difference.[4] It is not as if God created us once and for all, wound us up like little toy cars, and then released us to go as far as we could before we need his help again. Rather, God is constantly recreating us, continually calling us out of the primordial nothingness whence we came.

For this reason, I don't think that there is any meaningful difference between creation and providence, for in both we sit on the very edge of chaotic nothingness, suspended

---

3   Boris Pasternak, Dr. Zhivago, trans. Max Hayward and Manya Harari (Pantheon Books, 1958), 75.

4   Throughout this book I assume a historical fall that was preceded by an unfallen world in which humans and animals dwelt at peace with each other and with God. However, there are good reasons to discredit the historicity of the fall, chiefly that animal death and suffering predate the existence of humans.

only by the will of an inscrutable God. This truth is, quite simply, terrifying.

And at times the precariousness of our existence seems so real. I remember the spring of my senior year, when my emotional life seemed to be one massive Gordian knot, chaos crossed over itself in a thousand different directions, looped, knotted, tangled, unbreakable and screaming. As that internal chaos grew ever more deafening, it dragged me slowly and inexorably toward nothingness. Long before I was almost overwhelmed by the temptation to kill myself, I felt void of the desire to live. Several times I caught myself thinking that my greatest aspiration in life was to die a Christian death. I fantasized about my funeral. Even now, on the days when death seems a distant possibility, the presence of emotional turmoil is enough to crumple me and bring me, powerless, to tears, at the mercy of whoever is willing to withhold judgment and listen during the time it takes for me to figure out what I'm feeling and why.

As with death, there is nothing good that can be said about chaos itself. Chaos is merely that state that comes before the meaning and clarity called light.

In Your Light

In your light we see light.[5]

L ight is like truth in that the brightest lights—the sun, the moon, the shining stars—do not depend on us, but the lesser lights—streetlights, house lamps, blazes—do. So too, we have some degree of power over the truths that rule our lives. He can cheat on his spouse, negating the truth of their marriage. She can truthfully count her hours at work, affirming the truth of her vocation. But we have no control over the greater truths of our existence. Although we deface ourselves, we cannot erase the image of God; though we curse him, we cannot obliterate our maker; though we distance ourselves from all people, we cannot wriggle free of divine love. And though we relentlessly vaunt our knowledge, thinking that all things can be measured with our grubby hands and scientific minds, we find ourselves enshrouded in a mystery penetrable not by human reason, but by divine wisdom alone.

When on earth did we start thinking we could actually know anything? Before I had even considered epistemology, the study of knowing, my high school philosophy teacher

---

5   Psalm 36:9

had half-jokingly told us of his epistemology students gripping their chairs in fear of unknowing. And while I doubt that the paralysis of fear is the right response to humanity's epistemic predicament, it seems to me that the chair-grippers understood the import of what he was teaching: all they thought they knew was dubious. Many would oppose this broadly postmodern impulse on theological grounds, as if it was philosophy that had pointed us all in the wrong direction and the job of theology was to appeal to what we had always known to set us right again. But an argument for humanity's epistemic bankruptcy can and should be made on theological grounds: it follows from the ontological difference between God and human beings, not to mention our corruption after the fall. It preserves the Pauline assertion that salvation is not merely legal but also epistemic (Christ, the Wisdom of God). And it safeguards the truly Christian idea that knowledge is not a solitary endeavor, but a relational act. "In your light, we see light."[6] The gospel hangs on the assertion that, in Christ, believers are drawn out of epistemic darkness into the true knowledge of Christ. Christians leave epistemic oblivion, but we never transcend epistemic dependence.

The primary manifestation of this dependence on God for the light of knowledge comes in the form of our dependence on the church. Were it not for that ancient collective of followers of the Way, who, though splintered and broken and conflicted and confused, perpetuated the gospel of God's grace through generation after generation of despair, my grandparents would never have come to faith in Jesus. Without them, my parents would not have believed and,

---

6   Psalm 36:9

in turn, taught me to believe. To be sure, I owe my bare existence to my father's loins and my mother's womb. But I also owe my hope to my parents, who patiently taught me to believe in Christ. How, to paraphrase St. Paul, would I have learned of Jesus if no one taught me? And how would anyone be able to teach me unless they, in turn, were taught?

Belief, however, is not a one-and-done mental act, but a day-by-day submission to the reality given us (never possessed by us, as though we were the real knowers) by Christ. Perhaps—and I don't say this tongue-in-cheek, but as a real possibility—you might be able to sustain your belief with nothing other than your faculties of reason and dogged determination to think what you have always thought. But I find myself often needing a large amount of help.

It's August 2017, and my fiancée Laurie and I are spending a week with my family in Avalon, New Jersey. The two of us are sitting on the grass outside the public library, when sustained frustration that my new headphones aren't working turns into a full-fledged panic attack. For forty minutes, I writhe and struggle under Laurie's gentle, non-coercive hands, shocked at my own despondency and shaken to the core as suddenly as an unforeseen earth-quake. The cause of all this commotion? A near-complete inability to see reality, a losing of touch with the central truths of my person and of the world. Some time during this desperate struggle against inner twilight, I ask her as I often do: "What's true?" She responds: "I love you, I see you, I'm going to take care of you, all this is just weather. It doesn't bother me."

"It doesn't bother me." This phrase is particularly help-ful because it reminds me that my inner turmoil, utterly dark though it may be, cannot even cast a shadow of doubt

on her love for me, nor can it even disrupt her mood. While
I, in my distress, oftentimes find myself extraordinarily vulnerable to whatever she says to me, that same distress does
not discourage her. At the moment where my entire capacity to know is contingent, she remains invulnerable and is
able to speak the truth of Christ to my heart. Conversely,
I also am able to encourage her when she is discouraged.

Laurie's steadfastness testifies to a truth just as fundamental as the truth that we cannot know anything of
our own accord: reality does not depend on us. Just as the
celestial motion of the greater and lesser lights continues
utterly independent of our futile human attempts to shelter
ourselves, both from their reality and the reality of their
maker, so too the truths most fundamental to reality, given
to us in Christ, remain despite (and in the case of the cruci-
fixion, because of) our urgent attempts to extinguish them.
We cannot obliterate the truth of God any more than we
can obliterate the truth of ourselves.

Thus, when I think of the interplay of light and darkness
in my own story and the stories of others, darkness is not
an independent reality, but a mere obscuring of the light
that is always there.

Nakedness

*And the man and his wife were both
naked, and were not ashamed.*[7]

Just a few weeks before going to the hospital the spring
of my senior year, I posted an anonymous one-page
reflection on my college's forum wall. I titled my reflection, "Living with a Devil." It was penned with a desperate
candidness not uncommon to those on the outskirts of my
college community who characteristically refuse to accept
theological justifications for their suffering. In hindsight, I
see that piece as a last gasp, a desperate attempt to articulate
the precarious fight for life my fragile existence had become.
But, truthfully, it was more than just a cry for help; it was
a prophetic message to a community that did not seem to
recognize the dire situation of the mentally ill in its midst.

I had finally, and belatedly, begun to expose the terror
that I faced on a daily basis to the light of community. I
had long believed the lie that the people who asked me
how I was doing didn't actually care. To be sure, I've seen
many ask "How are you?" unthinkingly and instinctively, as
a mere extension of a greeting. I've since learned that when

---

someone asks how I'm doing, they often do genuinely care about my well-being, even if they may not be expecting to hear anything other than "fine" or "good." Even so, becoming vulnerable about my mental illness that spring was not an easy road and was fraught with pains and misgivings. Here is one conversation I had with an acquaintance:

Luke: How are you?

Henry: Well, I've been depressed a lot.

L: I'm sorry to hear that.

H: How are you?

L: I'm good, thanks. You know, when you said you were depressed, it took me aback.

H: Why's that?

L: I think of depression as something very personal, and I'm surprised that you decided to share it with me.

H: Hmm. I feel like our community struggles a great deal to be vulnerable, and I'm trying to change that.

L: But surely vulnerability can be misused. I've seen a lot of people simply spill their guts in the name of vulnerability. There's a way of being vulnerable that adds to the pain that is already being experienced, instead of purging it.

Even though I didn't think I had overshared, I knew all too well what Luke was alluding to. At its core, unhealthy vulnerability is sharing one's pain in a way that repels others instead of bringing them near. Harmful vulnerability creates monologue instead of dialogue, alienating both the sufferer and the hearer. In fact, it is not actually vulnerability, since it does not invite the deeper knowledge that only comes with questioning and conversation, but instead shuts off conversation by intentionally speaking beyond the interpretive horizons of the listener. This quasi-vulnerability is a dysfunctional defense mechanism against the pious platitudes that are commonplace at the college I attended, a two-faced manner of being invulnerable to the words of others precisely by disclosing one's suffering in the most extreme terms. How dreadful that a means of alienation could pose as true self-revelation. Tragically, both platitudes and this defensive self-disclosure lead to the bifurcation of a community into two collectives: those who subtly pride themselves on having it together and those who subtly pride themselves on not having it together.

The desire to isolate and guard ourselves from others lies deep within our bones, no less in Christian circles than elsewhere. So often when we think of praising God or serving the world, we forget that true love requires genuine self-disclosure, and that this in turn entails the vulnerability of dialogue. To "serve" someone while being invulnerable to them is a terrible insult. I think of the widespread practice of short-term mission trips—often, they allow participants to experience difference (a new language, a new cuisine, the city) without themselves being changed by the experience. Trips like these can make short-term missionaries and the organizations that send them *less* vulnerable than before by creating an artificial dialogue in which they interrogate the people and the places to which they are sent while remaining blissfully invulnerable. For to see truly is to be changed by the seeing. How can one possibly see a country in the global south without having one's habits of consumption called into question? Yet we manage to do so all the time. In doing this, we preclude the other from disclosing herself precisely by placing ourselves invulnerably above reproach. If we are not willing to be known by those whom we seek to know, we cannot understand them, much less love them.

I long for genuine vulnerability. I long for a world in which we who suffer could share our experiences humbly and candidly with neither shame nor false pride. More comprehensively, I hope for a day in which everyone will be able to truly self-disclose and draw others closer in the process. These longings, according to scripture, look both forward and backward—forward to the day in which true unity in Christ will be realized, but backward to that moment where Adam and Eve were naked and not ashamed. Their nakedness was both their vulnerability and their innocence: vulnerability because there was nothing separating them from each other, innocence because they knew no need of such a separation. Now, in the interim between the lost garden and the coming city, nakedness is permitted in marriage, but we have lost our innocence and must toil endlessly to be genuinely vulnerable with each other. When will we finally be able to speak without hurting? When will we cease to harm each other through our nakedness? When will our nakedness again reveal the truth of who we are, instead of being a weapon that we wield against others—and ourselves? Whatever Christ meant by saying that there would be no marriage in heaven, I hope desperately that he meant that we would be vulnerable to all heaven and earth in an analogue to the nakedness of marriage.

Sadly, Luke and I have seldom talked since. I told him I had been in the hospital, to which he nodded and gave me a hug. But tragically, it seems that our conversation proved the end of a dialogue, not the beginning of one. And the questions our interactions raised remain constant, existential questions for me. How can I share the desperation common to my experience without alienating those to whom I speak? How can I convey it in a way in which they are drawn into my narrative and I into theirs? How can my nakedness empower their voice instead of robbing it?

The Order of Things

And there was evening and there
was morning, the first day.[8]

There is a paradox deep in the heart of nature. On the one hand, it is not arranged according to human logic. On the other, it has an order that is simply stunning. How is it that ants work so efficiently toward the goal of sustaining their colony, an outpost of life against the trampling of human feet and the many dangers of the ground? Where did the elegant geometry of celestial bodies originate? How to explain the curiously photogenic drooping of tree limbs, spreading a canopy of leaves like a shawl over the forest's undergrowth? Who can bear to explain away an oxbow lake, a hairpin turn that came to be long before asphalt highways and their human creators? So often we have understood this order as an appeal to reason, an inductive argument: such order cannot come without a divine Creator. Surely such beauty is not primarily the stuff of reason, but the kindling for a fire of wonder. To reason is to view the conclusion as an object, but to wonder is to see oneself as subject, captive to an immortal mystery.

---

8   Genesis 1:5

Paradoxically, scripture teaches that the order both underlying and deep within creation is the foundation for human existence. That order is temporal: just as God rested on the seventh day, so the Israelites were to rest. And just as the Israelites rested on the seventh day, so the bride of Christ is to enter the sabbath rest of God. The order is also spatial: God placed human beings within a garden, a tended piece of land with borders—the original division between civilization and wilderness. It is moral: God created fruits good for eating, but also a forbidden fruit. Other orders we can only dream of may have existed within the unfallen world: relational, numerical, astronomical, spiritual, doxological...

Creation is not merely the sudden existence of creatures *ex nihilo*, but the bringing of order to all created things, the victory of order over chaos and its banishment to the outermost reaches of the universe.

And it was good.

Order is the coming together of necessity and freedom. Necessity, because order has authority over the shape of things. Freedom, because this authority does not exist for its own sake but for the sake of the things that it orders. Necessity, because repetition is necessary for order to be intelligible. Freedom, because rote repetition that allows no newness is a form of death. And all have suffered an overdose of either necessity or freedom. Mere necessity is the mindless bureaucrat whose life is a mindless regurgitation of the same statutes, a mechanical application of the same rules over and over again. Mere freedom is the hopeless artist, whose creative capacities are stifled, not enabled, by her lack of consistency. To be sure, we associate order more with the bureaucrat than we do with the artist. But in truth, order is not static, but dynamic. It goes by other names too: one of them is liturgy, the continual re-living of the same routines, the recitation of the same texts, the reformation of the same fallen bodies. Hold it too tightly and order will be crushed by law; hold it too loosely and order will fall prey to the fleetingness of desire. In short, order is a sweet spot between two extremes.

Much of my life is an existential search for order. It is the desperate struggle to call my internal giants by their right names and thereby to assign them their proper places and allow them to flourish or die as befits them. It is the quest to live rhythmically, yet not without innovation. An obvious truth: if you want to overcome depression, you have to sleep enough and eat well. To have order is life to me, but to be ruled by either law or wantonness is to die two deaths that are ultimately the same. While order is truly an existential necessity for me, the fact that order is embedded within the fabric of creation means that the ordering of life does not ultimately depend on me. In other words, order is transcendence ministered to me daily by creation.

Whether I like it or not, the sun will set eight hours from now. The birds will quiet, the stars will become visible, and the earth will be peaceful for a short time. Next month, the trees will lose their leaves, fluttering toward decomposition in a brilliant shower of gold, orange, red, and even purple. The fall rains and winter snows will come whether I desire them or not. Though humanity has made impressive progress in disrupting the rhythms of creation and the earth has produced some odd phenomena in response, we will never be able to disrupt the order of the world entirely. Were we to steer our own planet into the sun, Io would still orbit Jupiter with a beautiful, geometric consistency. Were we somehow able to destroy the sun, Alpha Centauri would still shine unabated. Were we to lay ruin to the unfathomably large Milky Way, millions of other galaxies would give forth their light, only visible from millions of leagues beyond our inestimably small human scope, but constant and inscrutably brilliant nonetheless. Order is transcendence. Whoever said that cleanliness was next to godliness was partially right, in that cleanliness is the ordered flourishing of a space. But cleanliness is the sort of order that depends on human beings, whereas the order closest to divinity depends not on humans, but on the mighty word of God.

The paradox of order is that it incorporates both necessity and freedom, bringing them into their fullest truths by integrating them. But the paradox of creaturely order is that while we are dependent on it, it is not completely dependent on us. I can counteract my body's natural tendency toward order by upsetting my circadian rhythm, eating disproportionate amounts of sugar (and that at odd hours), and lazing around for months on end before attempting to run a marathon. But even if I do this, I will not be able to transcend the order of creation which transcends me. Most immediately, my body will rebel against me, begging to be left to exist within its natural patterns. But should I resist its urgent pleas, I will be resisted by an external, transcendent rhythm of life. I cannot, like Moses, make the sun travel backwards across the sky, nor can I even do anything substantial to change the rhythmic hustle and bustle of the busy world around me. And, in most basic terms, I can never extract my experience from space and time, which impose an order on me all of their own.

The appropriate response to order is submission. I think of the man caught gathering sticks on the sabbath. Moses, unsure what to do with the transgressor, consulted God and was told to put him to death. Make no mistake—this is an utterly disproportionate punishment for a minor infraction. But understand Exodus within its cosmological context (i.e., the creation story of Genesis), and this transgression becomes a rebellion not only against the laws of the nascent theocracy of Israel, but an assault on the very fabric of being—the opposite of submission to God. To be sure, order involves creation as well; it is not only something that is imposed on humans, but something that is created by us. But, paradoxically again, the creation of order is a submission to its spirit, an acknowledgment that order itself transcends us and is guiding our feeble efforts toward it. It is this submission, not least, that was lacking in humanity's fatal fault.

The Fatal Fruit

*Of the tree of the knowledge of good
and evil you shall not eat, for in the day
that you eat of it you shall die.*[9]

Spring of my senior year. Day four of my week in the hospital. Loneliness and despair have sunk deep into me as I sink deep into them. I grapple with the cruel paradox that remaining in a multimillion dollar corporation supposedly designed for the sole purpose of healing the sick is in fact gnawing away the precious little life I have left. My new drug, Haldol, which was supposedly to help relieve my anxiety and stabilize my mood, puts me to sleep for fourteen hours per day and makes me groggy and miserable for the remaining ten. My hospital psychiatrist (not the psychiatrist I saw before and after being in the hospital), who has managed to combine this medication with another that it ought not to be paired with, shames me for my whirling, obsessive thoughts and suggests that I would fare better in a long-term inpatient program for sexual addicts. Something warns me not to believe him, but I am not even close to self-assured enough to ward off the screaming assault

---

9   Genesis 2:17

of shame that his indiscreet words precipitates. Only long afterwards will I realize how harmful his ministrations were to me that week.

I try to walk, but every time I pass someone in the hall, I fear I will harm them. Four people phone today; I can bear to talk to each of them no longer than five minutes before ending each conversation out of guilty exhaustion. Laurie will later tell me that when we finished talking that day, she threw her phone on her bed and wept for despair. My father calls from the Netherlands and realizes that I'm not getting better and that his or my mother's intervention will be necessary to get me out of the hospital. They book her transatlantic ticket within hours. Nobody on the phone knows what to say, and I least of all. A chronically anxious patient who is a nurse by vocation asks me if I have thoughts of hurting someone else, "because that's scary as shit." With whatever tired concentration I have left, I look her in the eye and lie, "No." Even though my mind is as murky as it's ever been, it's still clear to me that her rabid anxiety's focus on mine will aggravate it, thereby doing the impossible—making my time in the hospital more miserable than it already is.

Increasingly, my thoughts turn toward destruction. A bald, muscular police officer visits the ward, and I think of touching him sexually, but not in any particular way. My inchoate urges—sexual, aggressive, harmful to others and myself—are inscrutable. There is nothing of desire in them. Those thoughts which tell me to clutch at a woman's breast have no libido; the thoughts that tell me to strike the case worker have no real enmity in them. For to truly desire to hurt another would require me actually considering them as persons, and right now I can consider them only as phantoms surrounding the screaming core of my consciousness. To hurt them would be simply an externalization of the pain I am not feeling, not a personal act against them. Of course, such a harmful act would be a profound insult to their humanity, as it would use them as a means to my own self-destruction, which I am drawn to almost irresistibly. I feel like I am on a steep, slippery slope. At the top is well-being, but I am sliding down the glacial scarp, falling into the abyss into which our first parents fell. Everything in me is self-destruction, and my dark thoughts reflect an urge toward nothingness that can only be withstood with great effort—a truly nihilistic alignment that proceeds from the fall.

One of the criteria for personhood is existence within a moral landscape.[10] In scripture, God's first commands to humanity (to be fruitful and multiply, and not to eat of the tree of the knowledge of good and evil) predate the fall. Thus, our human ancestors went about their days with the possibility of evil, in a state that Augustine calls *posse peccare*. The scriptural ideal for human flourishing is not a simple transcendence of laws, either human or divine, but deliberate, liturgical choices to live an ordered life within the constructs of laws which tend toward human flourishing (although, curiously, redeemed humans will ultimately be in a state of *non posse peccare*—will this not quench our personhood?). So the fall is not the introduction of moral principles, but their violation—and that with cosmic consequences. Whereas the first humans lived in a level moral landscape in which their choices were not impaired

---

10 I owe this insight to Dr. Mark Talbot, a beloved philosophy professor.

by previous wrongdoing, we now make our choices on a sharp moral iceberg, on the slopes of which even our best intentions slip almost inevitably toward self-destruction. Law existed before the fall and was cursed by it. Unfallen (if one can even speak in such a hypothetical), I would have had to look far and wide for a means of self-annihilation. Now I glide toward self-destruction effortlessly and expend a lifetime's worth of effort trying to return whence I fell.

Seemingly against all odds, I was able to hang on until my mother set foot in my hundred-yard long dungeon two days later. Two days after that, she pulled me out of the hospital against medical advice. While the weeks and months ahead would be a continuation of the same desperate, day-by-day struggle against the grain of my own fallenness, I was no longer alone. I was and am no longer solely responsible for halting my fall toward the abyss. And I've made a lot of progress since that dark fourth day in the hospital. Even though the horn of a passing train, the sharpness of a pocketknife and the roar of a semi in the opposite lane are sometimes enough to make me tremble, thoughts of ending my life are most often distant possibilities, not pressing threats. Thoughts of hurting others are now a rare occurrence. With the help of family, friends, and my dear fiancée, I have found my foothold on the iceberg and remain planted there. Until when? I do not know.

With fallenness comes a new contingency, the possibility that every moment we will reap ever more of the consequences of our own actions and God's curse upon them. The greatest of these consequences is called shame.

Shame

The man and his wife hid themselves
from the presence of the LORD God
among the trees of the garden.[11]

One of my greatest daily challenges is to look Laurie in the eye.

I'm serious. For me, the keys to a good greeting that my father drilled into me when I was a child—firm handshake, look them in the eye, smile—are small potatoes. It's easy for me to communicate genuine love to people I'm meeting for the first time. When I look into their eyes, I see some mixture of uncertainty, goodwill, joy, sadness. Greeting them lovingly is simple, not least because I know the limitations of their knowledge of me. Our understandings of each other are directly proportional to the depth of our shallow, piecemeal interactions. Even if one of us in a moment of bravery manages to be genuinely vulnerable to the other, that self-disclosure will most likely remain an isolated instance in a relation of well-meaning mutual ignorance. For them, I am a face that will likely appear in their cluttered lives a handful of times at most, a string of

---

11 Genesis 3:8

expressions and words witnessing to a deeper personal reality that they have no access to. I no longer live in the fear (or sometimes the hope) that these distant friends will be able to intuit my situation; if I do not tell them something, they likely will not know it. There is great security in privacy. In most of our relationships we remain largely unknowing of the other and largely unknown. There are few people on this earth that I cannot hide from, and it's their knowledge of me that I fear.

Why? Because to be in a profound relationship is to be subject to the questioning of the other. I can choose what I share with someone else; I cannot determine what her questions of me will be. Faced with a question, I can decide to refuse to answer it or to lie, but this would be to negate the value of the asker and the truth of our relationship. The remaining option—to answer honestly—requires the defenselessness of nakedness. For in answering vulnerably, one is completely subject to the care and love of the asker. Thus, honesty has more to do with courage than with factuality. Anyone can list off facts about herself willy-nilly: "I don't like cheesecake, I listen to the Beatles on a regular basis, I am the eldest of three sisters." But to allow the private caverns of one's person to be explored by another through the acts of questioning and answering— that takes an uncommon courage. In the courage required for self-disclosure we see the paradox of fallenness: it takes extraordinary effort to return to the fundamental truths of our very beings.

No sooner have Adam and Eve eaten of the forbidden fruit than they attempt to cover themselves. I say attempt because, as the rest of Genesis 3 shows, Adam and Eve's attempt to hide themselves both from each other and from

God is futile—if anything, it compounds their preexisting guilt. Nonetheless, they go about hiding with reckless abandon, first sewing loincloths out of fig leaves, then hiding from God among the garden trees and finally hiding their own guilt behind blaming another—first the man blames the woman, then the woman blames the snake. Shame is present at the very beginning of fallenness and, not unsurprisingly, it is shame that has sustained fallenness. Which is the greater problem, that we have sinned or that we are too afraid to admit our wrongdoing to ourselves, let alone to God? Shame is guilt wreaking the full extent of its harm as the guilty one refuses dialogue, voids others from her inner realities, and attempts to live a futile existence outside of all community.

The worst effect that reading the Genesis account, or for that matter the entire woeful story of the Old Testament, could have on someone is engendering a false sense of security through the blame of those ancient sinners. Are we not tempted to blame Adam and Eve's foolish rejection of divine law, blissfully forgetting our own futility in the love of God and neighbor? To be sure, their story is sordid, but ours is no better. So often, our blame of others is simply a concealment and extension of our own shame. Our frustration at the faults of others often has little to do with their actions and the consequences of those actions and much to do with our own moral failings, hardness of heart, and foolish ignorance. And if we are indeed culpable, then the story of the fall and of those guilt-ridden Israelites is our story indeed: their guilt is no different than ours, their shame our own.

But just like those Israelites, we have a choice: to live in shame or not. I think of that orgy at Shittim, when the

Israelite men, as the story goes, forsook the worship of God for hedonist debauchery with the Midianite women. According to Numbers, 24,000 died that day. Perhaps the Israelite men were simply bewitched by their own lusts and fell prey to their sexual urges. But I can't help but wonder whether the underlying reason for their rebellion against their wives and their God was their desire to escape their own guilt; in other words, the orgy was caused by their shame. Did they not want to escape the daily litany of animal blood spilled on their behalf, constantly accusing them of their own wrongdoing and unworthiness before an angry God? And what could be a better holiday from a rigorous sacrificial religion than a heathen fling with a sultry young Midianite? Thousands of years later, our generation has the same dilemma as those lusty Israelites. Will we choose to drown our own guilt in the fake intimacy of pornography, that demon that makes intimacy a sham? If we are to triumph over both the subtle and extreme forms of sexual degradation that unceasingly wage war against our bodies and especially the vulnerable bodies of sex slaves, we must strive with all of our beings to relate to each other in earnest. We must resist the temptation of voyeurism and accept the challenge of being known. In a sense, prayer—the deepest form of intimacy—is not a holy but an unholy act, in that it simply cannot be done effectively without a recognition of our unworthiness: any form of prayer that confirms our illusions of holiness is arguably more abominable than that great orgy.

Even though I would currently like to think myself relatively invulnerable to sexual immorality, I am still susceptible to its germ—shame. I fight the battle for true vulnerability every day, and oftentimes I fail. I catch myself preferring to face away from Laurie as she sits next to me and talks, and wonder why. Am I unwilling to give her attention? No, but I'm unwilling to feel seen by her. Until I overcome this stubborn unwillingness, this echo of the first fall, I can do no good thing.

The First Glimmer

He shall strike your head, and
you will strike his heel.[12]

<u>TRIGGER WARNING</u>: This chapter contains references to sexual violence which may be triggering to survivors.

He is a wandering bard, devastated by the wrongdoing of his neighbors. He walks the streets haggard and unshaven and sees the undoing of his own country before his very eyes. Just to the right, those husky troublemakers from the next village over are carrying off the village midwife, dragging to her own rape kicking and screaming. Two nights ago, he overheard the plundering of his childhood friend's house; powerless against the man who held a knife to his neck, his friend could only watch his home and hearth desolated. And worst of all, young Hannah, who used to walk to the market each morning with a basket of goat cheese under her arm to sell, went missing without a trace two months ago. No one can find her, and though her older brother does his best to persuade the town elders into starting a proper investigation, they prove unsympathetic.

---

12 Gen. 3:15

Didn't he know that they were otherwise occupied? One elder runs a vineyard, for which he hired the street whelps, paying them a sliver of a proper wage. Another fancies himself a weekend prophet. He stands in the square and declares that what God wants most is for the townspeople to submit to the agricultural tycoons, who combine farm after family farm until they have a stranglehold on the village's production of food. "Doesn't he have two brothers who run large farms?" the common folk wonder. But no one dares challenge him. Figuring out what God is really saying is a tricky business, particularly if you think that he's saying something different than what that wealthy mogul down the road thinks.

Habakkuk sighs, wondering whether today will be the day that he finally gives up on God, because God certainly seems to have packed up and left this village a long time ago. Millennia before those enlightened free-thinkers dubbed themselves atheists, Habakkuk considers a choice no less radical: whether or not to stop holding out hope for that mysterious deity whose praise has been the liturgy of his mother's mothers and father's fathers for as far back as anyone can remember. Prophecy, after all, is standing apart from the masses, and Habakkuk anxiously weighs whether to keep his head down and keep trying to eke out a living in one of the worst neighborhoods for miles around, or to try to purge faith from his aging body and to tell all his neighbors that this time, God really has quit on them. He can't decide.

The next day, he has a fight with his brother-in-law. It starts when Habakkuk makes an unguarded comment about his sister and backs down only when the beloved of his own sister threatens to pull a knife on him. As he walks home, Habakkuk swears under his breath. And as he slams the door to his boarded-up house, he finally lets it all go and yells, "God, where the hell are you? Is *this* how you treat those you love? Am I the only one who sees the problem with this town, while you sit in heaven and can't seem to give a damn?" Not exactly the stuff of a pious complaint, but Habakkuk doesn't care anymore. There's more desperation than devotion in his rant; his respect for the divine is no longer articulable in liturgy and now draws on the throaty gutturals of Hebrew, the coarseness of which puts Anglo-Saxon expletives to shame. His fury gives way to dread when God, silent for so long, picks that opportune moment to let him know that within a couple of years it won't be the neighborhood hooligans but the vicious Babylonians marauding through his street. Somehow, Habakkuk finds the boldness to retort, "isn't that more unjust than leaving this dump of a town to rot under the weight of its own violence?" "No," God thunders again, "because the Babylonians too are going to get what's coming to them." And God plants a dream in the soil of Habakkuk's conflicted heart: one day, the violent will be silenced by the knowledge of God, which is to say that violence itself will be dissipated by a deep calm that transcends it. One day—*that Habakkuk won't even live to see*—both those small-town rapists and the foreign hordes sent to punish them will be forced to do the one thing most contrary to their pillaging ways: to strip themselves of brutality just long enough to listen to the holy silence that has outlasted them.

The book of Habakkuk is, more than anything else, a book about the transformation of one person. He begins as a confused doubter, distraught at the current lack of justice right before his eyes. God's first answer throws him into a deeper confusion—how, Habakkuk wonders, is it right for God to combat injustice with more injustice, to replace the petty village ruffians with the Babylonian hordes? But the book in his name ends with one of the most stirring expressions of hope in the scriptures. Even though, Habakkuk sings, the very plants that sustain his fragile life are pillaged ruthlessly, even though the fledgling Israelite nation is steamrolled by a military force of apocalyptic proportions, even though disaster will come to everything he holds dear and he will not even live to witness the beginning of the restoration of his homeland, yet he will hope in God. Habakkuk survives on what might be called bare hope, since he knows that he will not experience the realization of his hope. His is a hope founded on the ground of despair, which offers the firm knowledge that things could not possibly be worse and the assurance that no matter who you are and where you are found, you can experience the same radical hope.

This bedraggled prophet is as relatable for me as anyone else in scripture. The nakedness, the absurdity of his hope, reminds me of my time in the hospital or, indeed, much of my extended depression this last year, in which much of the time the only hope I could hold was that *things would not always be this way.* That the current desolation of my mind had a limit—while the destruction was astronomical, reconstruction was always possible. That how I felt today did not dictate how I would feel three months from now. That one day I would finally be properly medicated and thus be capable of going about my day-to-day life with a measure of joy approximating that of a mentally healthy human being. That I would not always fantasize about my self-destruction, that the dark ponderings of my mind would one day be dissipated by the light of love and that those inscrutable, mighty domains of my soul would fix themselves on the good and draw me toward it just as powerfully as they now drag me toward oblivion. Hope, by nature, is most compelling when all of creation seems to scream in despair, as it did that pitch-dark week in the hospital, as it did for the lonely prophet Habakkuk, as it did in the very moments when creation foundered into nothingness.

As the woman and the man hang their sorry heads after precipitating millennium upon millennium of suffering and alienation through their singular act of rebellion, the tone of the human epic seems to have been set. Human history is to be a tragedy of cosmic proportions, in which the original fall from grace dooms all descendants of the guilty pair to a life of utter oblivion, and in which consciousness will inevitably scuttle into the abyss from whence it came. As the cosmos faces nothingness, despair reigns supreme. Yet in one moment—a moment paralleled precisely by the absurdity of the resurrection after the desolation of the cross—there is a gleam of hope. It is hope hardly defined, fuzzy around the edges like an old photograph, but it is still hope. The serpent whose beguiling words pushed humanity into darkness will be defeated once and for all *through* the guilty couple themselves. Through the sufferings of the woman, the guilty scapegoat of much of the Christian tradition, the great enemy will be destroyed. Even though she has been condemned to death, she is soon after named Eve, "because she was the mother of all the living."[13] And, impossibly, the cause of hope lives on. Just moments later, Adam and Eve are driven out of the garden to their new

---

13   Genesis 3:20

existence of tears and groaning. Soon their eldest will kill his younger brother from spite. But that first hope survives throughout the weary pages of Genesis and indeed all the sorry story of the Old Testament, which more than anything else is the story of a people exiled not from the holy city but from the garden, not only from the land but from its maker. The hope *will not* die; history must stretch to include its fulfillment. The human narrative will no longer be an ineluctable descent from bliss into despair; for the word of hope must be fulfilled. And, even as the prophets of the Old Testament expand the hope with utopian visions of the reconciliation of God to his creation, the entire weight of human existence will continue to rest on that first promise: "he will strike your head, and you will strike his heel."[14]

---

14   Genesis 3:15

The Priests

*Why, O Lord, do you stand far off? Why do
you hide yourself in times of trouble?*[15]

It was week three of the intensive Christian outpatient
program I attended after coming out of the hospital,
and I was puzzled. The program had indeed been excellent.
The therapists were very helpful and, since there was only
one other person participating in the program, gave me a
lot of attention. Their kind, patient gazes and attuned ears
allowed me to pay attention to the thoughts hiding in the
darkness of my heart, twisting in a thousand knots since the
beginnings of this depression five months ago. Thanks to the
counselors, I was able to feel the emotions I had long since
become numb to: anger, sadness, guilt, shame, disgust. No
longer would they remain inchoate, eating at my very being
in secrecy. Now I could name them for what they were, feel
them as they came into me and filled me with themselves,
express them as they wished, and thus be free of them. Even
the art therapy sessions, which I had at first written off as
quixotic and unnecessary, proved to be helpful. My regular
psychiatrist had started me on a pair of medications with

15   Psalm 10:1

an almost immediate payoff. But curiously, faith seemed to play no role in the program. The therapists themselves rarely spoke of God unless one of the patients brought him up first. We didn't pray in session, heard no scripture, and spoke little of our involvement in local churches. I had chosen this program specifically because it was a Christian program. Why did spiritual practices not play a role in it?

While I couldn't understand why we didn't pray or read scripture in session, the truth was that *I didn't mind*. Even in the process of healing from the spiritual gashes I had sustained over the last five months, I felt no less abandoned by God. In the past, I had called my depressions doubt, guilt, seasons of sowing, or seasons of legalism, and I called my recoveries spiritual awakenings. My most recent depression, comprehensive in its scope, had obscured the presence of God so entirely that, even in my recovery, I believed God to have abandoned me completely. I was relieved that the counselors did not encourage me to try to translate my experience in the hospital and before into spiritual terms, because holding my vivid experience of God's absence in tension with a firm belief in God's unassailable presence seemed entirely impossible. And even now, months since then, I find myself mostly unable to believe many of the scriptural promises about God. How to believe that God cares for his own when I found myself on the verge of death despite the prayers of many who had heard of my struggle? How to think that God works all things for the good of those who love him when, if I look over the last two millennia, I see countless believers battered to bits, seemingly irrespective of their faith? I still don't see any way of squaring my experience of God's abandonment with the scriptural promise that God will never forsake those whom he has chosen.

The best I can do is hold them in an impossible tension. This is the tension of transcendence, the faith that something that I do not currently understand can resolve the seemingly irresolvable paradox that now offends my desire for a simple, logical response to every question under the sun. This, of all tensions, is one of the hardest to live in, for it requires one who has experienced anguish to affirm the reality of his own pain—and everything that that pain says about the God who at the very least allowed it to happen—and yet maintain the impossible notion that something outside of his experience of pain will have the last word. This stretching of the imagination and the will is precisely what faith in the resurrection of the Son of God requires.

But the early disciples of the risen Christ were not the first to live in that taut space between their own sorrows and the maker's love. Long before them were the Levites, who were before anything else ministers of the transcendence of God. Moses, the man responsible for their institution as the religious authorities of the young Israelite theocracy, was once approached by the people of Israel, who were overcome by the fear of a God far beyond them. They had heard his thundering on the mountain, and begged the wizened prophet to stand between their dreadful God and them because they could no longer bear to hear his voice. That ghastly fear of the numinous, the inability to reckon with the transcendent, is the psychological heritage of the entire Israelite priesthood, which seems to exist for the sole purpose of putting someone, *anyone* between the frail common folk and the thunderings of an oft-angry God, even if that unfortunate middle-man is every bit as undone by the slightest rumble of the divine as the people that he's supposed to represent. The Levites, incompetent though they were from Aaron, the great idolater himself, all the way down the line, forever stood between the woes of the people and God's promise to prosper them. Their hands held the knives that would slaughter masses of sacrificial animals. The same bloody hands also held the impossible hope that God, seeing the affliction of the slaughtered beasts as well as the downtrodden folk who brought them, would one day bring his people and even their livestock into fullness of life. The prophets were the great orators of the impossible, the priests were its ordinary enactors. Their very ministry stretched the fiber of the ancient imagination, asking it to believe that neither human tears nor animal blood would be wasted in the economy of God. Their actions appealed constantly to the transcendent, to that of which human reason can know nothing, to justify the ever-feeble hope that the only sovereign God would one day rescue his people from the only thing they had ever known—bitterness, hard labor, and tears. And impossibly, the priests stood as middle-men between a God they could not comprehend and a people for whom the *fear* of the Lord was not a pious longing but a daily reality.

Over the last couple of weeks, I have consciously avoided praying to God, using something, *anything,* to get my mind off God's silence. Were I to consider myself in the hands of a God whose will I could not understand, I would shake with fear. But—and I'm not at all sure that this is right—there is something deeply soothing about being in the position of a priest, mediating between God and humans. When I write, I am no longer scared. When I speak of my misgivings with God's mysterious ways, I no longer tremble. In the company of others, I am much quicker to come to terms with my ignorance of God. In all likelihood, it's because the acts of writing and speaking are cathartic for me and far easier than praying in isolation. But I also think it's because seeing another person in all of their paradoxes and complexities awakens me to their need of all the things for which I desperately grasp: the faith, hope, and love which are of God. As I interact with those who seek God and those who have all but forgotten him, the abstract gives way to the particular and the theoretical to the pragmatic. I worry less whether everything that I say about God is correct, because in the act of mediating the voice of God, I am finally able to forsake the fear of ignorance.

When both the Old Testament and the New speak of the people of God as a kingdom of priests, they mean that the people of God are meant to know God in the act of conveying his speech to another. The idea that faith should be kept private is absurd, not least from a pedagogical standpoint. How can one truly learn about something which one does not discuss? The professor who taught my evangelism class years ago claimed that spiritual maturity is measured by the extent to which one is willing to share one's faith with other people. True, but it is wrongheaded to think of speaking about God as an isolated act, as something that one does only as part of an evangelistic ministry. The trope of the street evangelist reinforces the assumption that speaking of God should involve the presentation of a ready-made message with the goal of converting people on the spot. But how could we think that God is so mercenary as to send his evangelists out on mission like newspaper sellers and cold-callers, as if participation in the kingdom of God were akin to subscribing to the latest magazine? Evangelism—the act of mediating the story of God to another person—is not a sales pitch. Furthermore, evangelism is not a competition. In many ways, the forms of evangelism that emphasize the self-evidence of the Christian faith and rely on apologetic arguments are the most caustic, not only because they lend to the knowledge of God a false immanence that owes much more to the Enlightenment than to the incarnation, but because they pit the arguments of the evangelist against the beliefs of the evangelized in a competitive debate in which the goal is not to love but to win. Evangelism at its best is a communal act of knowledge in which all members of the dialogue come to grips with their epistemic poverty and engage in the hard work of knowing a concealed God. It is not only the salvation of the unreached but the very faith of the mediator which is at stake—if she will not venture it in dialogue, it will shrivel and die.

Paradoxically, the act of mediating a mysterious faith to others works as a balm to the pangs of transcendence. It is not, as many have assumed, hypocritical to try to speak of a truth which one does not comprehend, so long as one is honest about one's ignorance. The peculiar blessing given to the priests is that they are not left to scrutinize the Lord by themselves, but that they may seek understanding precisely in the act of communicating that which they do not understand.

The Prophets

They will not hurt or destroy on all my holy mountain; for the earth will be full of the knowledge of the LORD as the waters cover the sea.[16]

Of all the slew of Old Testament prophets, there was not a single contented one in the bunch. Their office forbade it. Their task was to exhibit the distance between what was and what ought to be, and to put their very lives in the gap. In fact, many of them paid for the shortcomings of the nation with their blood, their martyrdom a final act of divine revelation to their calloused towns. They were occupational malcontents, and whenever their neighbors saw them, they wished that they would just shut up and get a real job. Of course, the prophets refused to be silent. Even if they had only seen the barest taste of what could be, that vision had lit a flame in them which would blaze all their lives. For they weren't simply pushed into mission by the desolation that either surrounded them or was just around the corner, but pulled forward by a utopian vision.

What was the substance of their utopia? What populated their vision of the future? Oftentimes, the world envi-

---

16 Isaiah 11:9

sioned by the prophets was an upheaval of what was and its replacement by its opposite, a photographic negative. Amos saw a society founded on the suffering of the oppressed and prophesied a day when justice would redeem the bottom-dwellers and the integrity of the nation they lived in. Isaiah saw a God determined to punish his people when they were too comfortable and prophesied that God would rescue them when all other hope was lost. Ezekiel grieved God's departure from the temple and, sure enough, the book in his name ends with God's return to the temple and to the heart of the Israelite nation that had forgotten about him. The darker the original photograph is, the brighter the negative. The darker the doom the prophet foresees, the brighter her celestial vision. The act most characteristic of God is the transformation of death into life, sorrow into joy, death into resurrection, dystopia into utopia. The darker the night, the brighter the morning. Of course, I can't help but speculate whether many of the prophets suffered from something like bipolar disorder.

My particular concoction of ailments has served to hollow my spirit into a spacious cavern. When the icy wind blows and the frosts of depression come, my inner being is as frigid and as desolate as the bare tundra. But when a fire is kindled, the same winds and the same space which made that interior so empty create a raging wild-fire.[17] Like the prophets, I swing vertiginously between two poles. Catastrophe and victory. Despair and hope. Numb-

---

17 I have been diagnosed with bipolar II. This means that I frequently experience mood cycling over the course of hours, days, weeks, and months. I also occasionally experience hypomanic episodes, which are much less severe and more enjoyable than the manic episodes characteristic of bipolar I.

ness and empathy. Vacillation and certainty. These states resonate respectively at the frequency of all that is wrong with and right with the world, or at least all that I can see. While I cannot claim that my words are inspired by God, my illness *feels* prophetic, in that it allows me to see the desolation of what is and the glory of what could be more clearly than those who live in a stable state of mind. The hollowed mind of someone suffering from mental illness can serve as a hallowed space in which God's damnation of the present and redemption of the future is manifest. In what might be termed bipolar prophetic discourse, darkness and light are not only conceptually but also psychologically interdependent. The darkness is inversely proportional to the light; the intensity of the light directly proportional to the intensity of the darkness.

However, there is a serious problem with this model: the substance of the future is not a simple negation of the present. To claim that the utopian future will be unlike the terrifying present is precisely to claim that the contents of the future are uncertain, because our ignorance of truth is an undeniable facet of the present. Deconstruction cannot miraculously turn into construction; apophatic theology cannot turn cataphatic. We cannot determine the contents of the future, which is beyond us, by simply negating the contents of the present or the past, for that is to posit a predictable inverse relationship between the actual and the potential. This works well as a heuristic device but poorly as a predictor of the future. More broadly, to think that the transcendent is simply that which is beyond the bounds of our understanding is fallacious. It is because we cannot comprehend the transcendent that its actuality bears no relation to the limits of our understanding. In brief:

visions of a future which are opposites of the present are not always reliable.

Thus, in order to understand prophetic discourse we must do the work of comprehending which ill is to be overcome by which good. I think of some of the Southern spirituals I love for their powerful imagery and striking harmonies— "Swing Low, Sweet Chariot," "In the Sweet By and By," "Go Down Moses." I most naturally imagine these songs to be about a spiritual escape from the toils of bodily existence, referring to an ephemeral promised land attained through death. If this is the case, then these songs will lull both oppressed and oppressors into a gnostic acceptance of the status quo by appealing to a fanciful future that has less to do with the biblical eschaton than a disembodied heaven. However, many suggest that the same black spirituals primarily concern release from slavery and oppression, not from the body.[18] In doing so, they appeal to

---

18   Consider these words by Frederick Douglass: "I did not, when a slave, understand the deep meanings of those rude, and apparently incoherent songs. I was myself within the circle, so that I neither saw or heard as those without might see and hear. They told a tale which was then altogether beyond my feeble comprehension; they were tones, loud, long and deep, breathing the prayer and complaint of souls boiling over with the bitterest anguish. Every tone was a testimony against slavery, and a prayer to God for deliverance from chains. The hearing of those wild notes always depressed my spirits, and filled my heart with ineffable sadness. The mere recurrence, even now, afflicts my spirit, and while I am writing these lines, my tears are falling. To those songs I trace my first glimmering conceptions of the dehumanizing character of slavery. I can never get rid of that conception. Those songs still follow me, to deepen my hatred of slavery, and quicken my sympathies for my brethren in bonds." From *My Bondage and my Freedom*, accessed 4/9/18, http://www.gutenberg.org/files/202/202-h/202-h.htm

the favor of a God who transcends their bondage and will one day obliterate it. It is far more powerful to sing these songs in hope of freedom and justice for the enslaved—both now and in the resurrection—than in hope of ephemerality.

Fundamentally, prophetic discourse is not so much about the dichotomy between present and future but about the continuity of the cause of faith, hope, and love. The Judeo-Christian utopian vision is founded in belief in a God who was and is and is to come. And this is just what the prophets proclaimed. Their prophetic visions of the future were not simply negations of the present but were rooted in their faith in the God who transcends history. The societal transformations they imagined were founded in the perpetual sovereignty of God and the faith that even though he had inexplicably allowed the present wrongs, they would one day be made right. For the prophets, continuity is primary; upheaval is secondary. The future will change precisely because God remains the same.

I see this mirrored within my own struggle for existence. While the thought of the sublation of the present into the reality of the future is comforting, hearing that the central truths of my existence transcend my ability to perceive them is far more helpful. To know that my belovedness does not depend on my ability to believe it, that there are those who will love me *no matter what*—this is far more helpful to me than the thought that my pain will one day end.

The Kings

Why have you despised the word of the
LORD, to do what is evil in his sight?[19]

<u>TRIGGER WARNING</u>: This chapter contains references to sexual violence which may be triggering to survivors.

In the summer, when the kings went off to war, the unlikeliest of kings met the unlikeliest of downfalls.

He had been faithful all those long years. From the moment that Samuel, in defiance of all expectations, had anointed him king, his valor had never wavered. David spared the life of Saul, his royal nemesis, not once but twice. Like Robin Hood, he played the noble rebel to a T. While fleeing that king, he became the model of virtue, not to mention one of the greatest poets the world has ever known. When the king who made himself David's archenemy finally died, David did not rejoice, but wept. He danced before the ark of God with abandon and built a reign on the steady foundation of his years of devotion and justice. Never before had Israel reached the grandeur enjoyed under King David, yet the prosperity attained under

---

19 2 Samuel 12:9

him would not outlast his grandson. David might have enjoyed his golden years, but instead, his old age became his downfall. The extent of David's fall is simply staggering. How does this great hero of the Old Testament, paralleled only by Moses in devotion and valor, stoop to murder and the vilest of adulteries? Do not imagine that David's sexual debacle is consensual adultery. No, David's command to bring Bathsheba to his bed is royal rape, sexual assault that transpired without Bathsheba's will.

How does this sin of sins come to be? I can think of one answer to explain it. It is listlessness that made David crumble; it is weariness that collapsed the greatest monarch the nation of Israel ever knew. By the time that he devastated Bathsheba's world just in order to lie with her, his short dark hair had already become a speckled silver, and his ruddy countenance had begun to wrinkle. The striking glint of his brown iris which had once drawn his band of misfit rebels together was now gone, and the corners of his lips were slightly downturned. While his body bore witness to his many years, an aging process far more destructive was taking place under his marbled skin. It manifested itself in the adultery and murder for which Israel's great lyricist was also renowned, but was not contained in those acts. David, in fact, had already fallen prey to it long before he stepped onto the palace roof. One might say that he lost his moxie, his nerve, his way. More precisely, David lost himself. The courage, daring, and honesty that had characterized his rebel years were not gone entirely, but they were crusted over by age and had long since become impotent.

Sometimes we talk about faithfulness as though it were a state in which one lives, a static remaining in the patterns and practices which constitute it. But faithfulness is not fundamentally static—it is dynamic. This point is of crucial importance. To be faithful in interpreting scripture is precisely to transpose the import of its contents onto the present day, allowing its words to say not less, but *more* than they have said before. To be faithful to one's spouse is not merely to keep oneself pure from adultery, but to live in a dynamic relationship that shifts and changes in accordance with love. Faithfulness to the nation under one's care is an ever-growing love for its people. Deviance is made out to be the great enemy of faithfulness; in reality, the greater foe is complacency. It is that withering force that overcame the greatest king of Israel and the nemesis that rises to do war with our best intentions before our eyes see the first light of each morning.

Even if we understand that complacency is a great adversary of a Christian life, do we address it properly? So often I have heard encouragements to "just try harder, believe harder, feel more, love more." But I don't think that this is the answer to complacency any more than attempts at self-humiliation are the answer to pride. One can't just humiliate oneself out of pride, because the act of consciously fighting pride leads to ever deeper layers of pride at one's ability to overcome the comparatively innocuous surface-level pride which one has disposed of. And if you try to just snap yourself out of listlessness, it probably won't work. Combatting pride or complacency or any vice, for that matter, requires a greater faith, a faith which transcends the besetting ailment that you face. If your faith centers around fighting one sin or another (as mine often has), then your faith needs to die as swiftly as possible and be reborn so that it is faith in Christ, not just faith in your own guilt or faith in your own capacity to fight off whatever the problem is. Complacency arises in the absence of motivation, and if you try to motivate yourself to overcome complacency for the sake of overcoming it, then you will likely fail. The good that you are motivated by must always be greater than that which you seek to change.

Even now, I struggle for motivation. My pace in writing has slowed over the last three weeks and I am impatient to have more words on the page. Today, I find my mind trying to whip and muzzle itself so that it produces optimally. Two pages is not enough; last week's speed will not do. I am desperate to be productive...but to what end? What am I trying to gain, other than to shut up that inner voice that tells me I am not doing enough? In my frantic drive to move forward, I am just as complacent as David, and life seems every bit as lonesome and boring. Paradoxically, my most apathetic and most harried moments share the same characteristic: they numb me to reality. What better defense against unease than either to sit bored and depressed on the palace roof, or to work oneself into oblivion? Both are convenient tactics for avoiding the inner malaise that drove one to those coping mechanisms in the first place. Either way, the world remains silent, and I deaf to it. In order to overcome this two-sided complacency, in order for work to be work and rest to be rest, my living and breathing must be anchored in a faith that transcends them and puts them in their proper place. If my work is to witness to something beyond my own strivings and misgivings, the truth must grab hold of my tired mind and point its efforts towards goodness.

Even David pointed to—or better, waved in the general direction of—God despite himself. Even though the Israelite monarchy was doomed from the very day his dreadful complacency brought Bathsheba to his bed, David witnessed to the true and coming king of Israel precisely through his failure. Though David fell prey to vice, the God who had put him on the throne was as vital as ever, and would not be defeated. The success of God's kingdom did not depend on the strength of the human kings who oversaw it, for David's central purpose was to witness to the kingdom that transcends the earthly and the king who would one day look his earthly judge in the eye and say that his kingdom was not of this world. Had David been dwelling on the coming kingdom, his complacency would have been overcome. Even so, the coming kingdom was none the worse for his transgression. Its true king, after all, was descended from Bathsheba and King David.

HERE BETWEEN
A Poem Trio
By Bryn Phinney

March 26, 2017, two Sundays before Easter
GENESIS 3:17-19

Crabapple by the Church

Your branches are cloven,
cursed at genesis.

One bite of ours
in fruit like yours,
was all it took
to break the whole genome
and leave your limbs barren,
mutant,
streaking for the sky
like back-
wards lightning.

Our bodies are charred
by simply breathing.

Ashes to ashes,
and dust to dust,
And yet,
somehow the current still flows
chlorophylled
beneath this twisted black bark.

All Things in Their Time

All things in their time,
like nine months longing for little purple toes
and full moon eyes—
her feet, his face—
lost in all this outer space.

Ancient words—
They say the whole world groans in waiting
for the Child's cry,
caught between contractions
like tree's bark torn
before the burst of green
crabapple tears.

April 17, the day after Easter
1 CORINTHIANS 15:3-4

And on the Third Day

Somehow
all it took were three short days.

The buds all burst their casings
while I was away
seeking to bury fear in
thick, Wisconsin beauty.

Seventy-two hours—
Good Friday to Easter evening,
and somehow
Winter rolled away.

A flood blew through, I heard,
and left its promise rainbowed
in every flowering thorn.

God Came Down

*He came down from heaven and by
the Holy Spirit was incarnate of the
Virgin Mary and became man.*[20]

Kristen stoops down toward the Chicago curb for the umpteenth time this afternoon. "Your sign says you feel homeless and ashamed," she says to the bedraggled stranger. "It's very brave to say that you're ashamed. Can you tell me more?" The mere giving of a sandwich will not do; she wants to be near this man, to hear him speak, to hug him. He sees the tattoo on her left forearm: a Lutheran cross, which represents her life-changing experience of grace when all hope seemed lost. Finding common ground in the ink embedded in their skin, they swap tattoo stories. From time to time, the man's gaze rises above the nearby gutter and his blue eyes flash. Even though his daily existence drags him toward hopelessness, the mere fact that he is willing to talk to Kristen makes it clear that he has not abandoned hope entirely.

I shift my weight to my right foot. Standing awkwardly

20   Nicene Creed, United States Conference of Catholic Bishops. Accessed Feb. 1, 2018. http://www.usccb.org/beliefs-and-teachings/what-we-believe/

above them, I feel ashamed because the man is ashamed and there is nothing that I can do about it. I try to focus on him but am preoccupied with my own awkwardness. How should I talk to him? Is it the right thing to do to get down on his level? Is giving him a sandwich going to do him any good in the long run? What if I was on the street like him? These questions have the same effect on me that headlights do to a deer: I am caught in them and do nothing. I catch most of the story that he tells, try to make eye contact with him, register the Starbucks across the street, and wonder how quickly we'll have to get back to the car before the time on the parking meter runs out.

All day long, he sees the bustle of the city around him. He wakes to the sight of suits and blouses flapping in the wind as their nameless wearers rush to their jobs. He goes to sleep to the frantic beeping of taxis swarming toward the darkness. In between, his waking day is a procession of leather shoes treading on his two squares of sidewalk. For every person who sees him, there are ninety-nine who don't. He sees a city that is self-assured in its animation and does not care about him. Its bustle drones on even as his existence is on the line. Others know Chicago by its sports teams, its press, its museums, or its blues bars. He knows it by the abandonment he suffers here.

From my journal back in February of my senior year, before the hospitalization, as I was in the throes of mood swings caused by taking my first antidepressant:

> The unchangingness of God is a helpful thought
> right now. I have gone through so many changes
> over the last six years or so—in health, in habits,
> in demeanor and location, yet God is still more

gracious and loving than I have perceived him to be. St. Julian's suggestion to pass through states of the soul as lightly as possible comes back to me again and again. This freedom is given us not because we have human reserve beyond the changes of mood and temperament, but because the root of our being is God, the unchanging one.

These words felt wrong even as I penned them, and since then they have grown ever less compelling. Why? Because contemplating the dispassion of God is not comforting to me when my very existence is turmoil. To look up from despair and to see a blissful God who remains unaffected by all sorrow is no help, at least not to me. I wonder if that is akin to looking up from the concrete slab you live on and seeing a suburbanite standing above you. A God who refuses to stoop to the tarmac cannot help us.

No, it is the contingency of Christ that is comforting.[21] If God is strictly beyond the suffering that we face by virtue of living on this earth, then the best that we are left with is an otherworldly hope that is utter despair for this life. If we must forever strain our necks to see the God above, whose countenance remains immune to our everyday passions, then we will not even want to know God—and why would we? We will not see God until our faces are level, which is to say, until Jesus stoops down in the dust and writes the truth of his coming on our encrusted minds. We will not know God until we see him *with* us. When Peter sees Christ beatified on the mountain, he imagines a God whose

---

21 *"Christ is contingency,"* writes Christian Wiman. *My Bright Abyss* (Farrar, Straus and Giroux, 2013), 16.

glory is the avoidance of pain and the grasping of power. Jesus sternly responds that Peter has it backwards: God in Christ has chosen not to be impervious to suffering, but to take on suffering and thereby to embrace those who suffer.

Is there any comparing my mental illness with the plight of the man on the streets of Chicago that day? I think not. The burdens we bear are non-quantifiable, and the feeble language we use to describe them can only ever name the pain, never measure its weight. But the burden of human flesh that Christ took upon himself is all-inclusive. To say that Jesus died on the cross is to say that he did not shrink from any sort of suffering, that he took on illness both mental and physical, that he embraced poverty of all stripes in order to embrace every impoverished person. To affirm the truth of the incarnation is to see that the heavens, which had forever seemed insensitive to human sorrows, now open to let down the omnipathic God. Perhaps Christ taking on human flesh, the mere fact of being born of Mary, is God's central act of compassion, of *suffering with*. For, long before he shouldered his cross, Jesus had already taken on mortal tissue, thus already condemning his mortal mind and his mortal tissue to death.

From "On a Theme from Julian's Chapter XX" by Denise Levertov:

> *The oneing*, she saw, *the oneing*
> *with the Godhead* opened Him utterly
> to the pain of all minds, all bodies
> —sands of the sea, of the desert—
> from first beginning
> to last day. The great wonder is
> that the human cells of His flesh and bone

didn't explode
when utmost Imagination rose
in that flood of knowledge. Unique
in agony, Infinite strength, Incarnate,
empowered Him to endure
inside of history,
through those hours when he took to Himself
the sum total of anguish and drank
even the lees of that cup:
within the mesh of the web, Himself
woven within it, yet seeing it,
seeing it whole. *Every sorrow and desolation*
He saw, and sorrowed in kinship.[22]

---

22 Denise Levertov, *Breathing the Water*, 68-69.

The Poor in Spirit

*God said to him, 'You fool! This very night your
life is being demanded of you. And the things
you have prepared, whose will they be?'[23]*

It is the beginning of the end for the first martyr in
Christian history. No sooner do the final words of Stephen's final speech leave his lips than he sees the high
priest straighten his aging body, raise his wizened fist to
the sky, and pronounce the ultimate Israelite indictment:
blasphemy! The accused watches as the damning word
echoes and resounds through the frenzied crowd. In the
great paradox of his martyrdom, Stephen is filled to the
brim with the power of the Holy Spirit, yet he is completely
powerless against the hordes that wash over him like the
fury of the wrathful God they thought they served. In the
blink of an eye, their feverish accusations turn to execution.
Stephen utters his final prayer and is gone in an instant.
A heroic end.

Stephen was not only the first martyr, but the first
deacon named in scripture. He is the foremost of those
chosen to bring the stigmatized into the center of the

---

23   Luke 12:20

growing church, yet a symbol of infamy for those outside the church. For Christ's most defining sermon had begun with the assertion that the poor (Luke) and the poor in spirit (Matthew) are at the very center of God's charity, and the deaconry was created precisely so that the Gentile poor would not be overlooked by the first generation after he ascended. Before he ever suffered the pains of persecution, Stephen was engaged in assuaging the pains of first-century widows. Long before he took up the cross of martyrdom, he had taken up the cause of the poor. Mere preaching was not enough for him: he wanted his deeds to be an enactment of Christ's preferential concern for the impoverished. Even before he suffered a disgraceful death at the hands of the priests, Stephen was no stranger to stigma. His travails amidst the lowest of the low had already earned him dishonor enough. As Paul's indictment of the ethnophobic apostle Peter and of the classist Corinthian church makes clear, stigma has been a force at work within the church ever since its inception. With every meal Stephen doled out, he worked uphill against the ingrained and inchoate forces of denigration, the same forces that would one day be his death, the same forces that the veneration of his martyrdom would overcome.

I've learned something about overcoming stigma in the church from another Stephen. He is the closest thing I know to a walking Bible: he has chapters of scripture committed to memory that I haven't even read in years. To be honest, I find almost anyone his age with a similar level of scriptural knowledge alienating. How to explain everyday existential angst to someone whose knowledge of scripture serves to immunize them to concerns that cannot be fit within a neat theology? How to try to speak with someone whose knowledge of scripture does not include an apprehension of the dire straits faced by its authors? How possibly to "do theology" with someone who has somehow managed to systematize the death of God? These are questions that confront me any time I'm speaking with one of my peers whose knowledge of scripture exceeds his capacity to empathize, but Stephen's acquaintance with suffering and compassion for those who suffer made me stop questioning his authenticity long ago.

Stephen's just been broken up with—the day after he had landed a job in the city where his girlfriend lived. He just found a group at his new church that he thinks he might fit into well, but they're on break for the summer and will only meet again months from now. His persistent concerns about vocation—what does God want him to do anyways?—continue, as does the depression that he's been in since last year. As I speak of my many misgivings with God, Stephen says something that would be a truism coming from almost anyone else: "Christ only preached to two types of people: the Pharisees and those who don't have it together. I'm glad you're in the second category." But it's not a truism coming from him. There's a firm gentleness in his voice that's compelling. I feel his compassion as we part ways. I wish he was still in the neighborhood.

To be poor in spirit is not to realize that one is unworthy of salvation. It is not a way of viewing oneself. Neither is it a prerequisite to being a recipient of God's grace, as though divine grace were something to be attained by an abstract cognitive act. You do not think yourself into spiritual poverty any more than you think yourself into any other sort of poverty. Not only is a desire for spiritual poverty odd, it is masochistic. The Beatitudes are descriptive long before they are prescriptive. They do not tell you the sort of person that you must be in order to get God's blessing; but they speak of the people God has decided to be *for* before anyone else. The phrase "blessed are the poor in spirit, for theirs is the kingdom of heaven" stands as a perpetual indictment of the church's reinforcement of worldly patterns of power and privilege, judging people for their sex appeal or their bank accounts...or their theology or repute in the church. If one can speak of privilege in the kingdom of God, it is precisely the inverse of the privilege perpetuated by the world. Blessed are the black and the homeless and the abused and the immigrants. Blessed are the women and the indigent and the veterans and the schizophrenics and yes, blessed are the queer. As I write I'm sitting next to a dear friend of mine who is often depressed, was abused as a child, is bisexual and doesn't know whether she can ever fit into a church again. Blessed is she—for if God doesn't care about her, why would he care about any of the rest of us? Because we have it together? If we dare to think that, we have made of Christ what the rest of the world has—a laughingstock—and have obliterated the most poignant part of his greatest sermon.

The great reversal, as Christ's upheaval of earthly power is often called, is precisely the placing of the most stigmatized people in every epoch into the epicenter of the kingdom of God.

On the Cross

*But when you grow old, you will stretch out your
hands, and someone else will fasten a belt around
you and take you where you do not wish to go.*[24]

I stopped praying for my friends and myself to be comfortable a long time ago. I used to pray that they would
do well on their finals, that they would have a good day or,
nebulously, that God would bless them. I prayed for my
family and myself when we were on vacation: that we would
have a good time. I prayed that I would be able to find a
particularly desirable book in the library. I prayed that God
would bless the food I had acquired through the suffering
of humans and animals alike. Now I never pray for those
things. Why? Because I don't think God cares.

No doubt this sounds like a dreadfully offensive state-
ment. Of course God cares, one might say, quoting Christ's
words about clothing the lilies of the field and feeding the
birds of the air. Truly God does care—but if Christ's words
about the birds and flowers are taken in context, they mean
first and foremost that God feeds the hungry and clothes
the naked. They don't mean that God becomes a cosmic

---

travel agent, arranging good holidays for the most privileged of his people, or that God is particularly concerned about the blessing of a sausage to someone's body. Incidentally, the blessing of food is often a prayer for nourishment through whatever is on the table. So why does the blessing of food not motivate us to source our nourishment equitably, to bless those who are part of producing food long before it reaches the shelves, let alone the table? Beyond food, I wonder how many of the things that western Christians ask God to bless are a direct and avoidable consequence of the suffering of the poor.

If God really answers prayer, I hope that he has greater things in mind than a nice vacation, parking spot, or meal. It seems to me that the most powerful thing that one can ever pray for is transformation, the type of transformation that results from Christ's kingdom coming to earth. We dare not pray for this transformation without praying that we ourselves be transformed. All too often, we imagine that the changing of our hearts will occur through some strenuous spiritual discipline of our own doing: maybe we will be more holy if we pray more, fast more, give more, go to church more. But even though the disciplines are ever so useful and are worth practicing, the process of transformation is often accomplished most expediently through suffering.[25]

To start a theology of the cross with the doctrine of substitutionary atonement—as if understanding this doctrine brings about salvation—is completely wrongheaded. In fact, to approach the cross with the abstract objectivity of a theologian is backwards. No, just start with the experience of Christ. Long before his body is hoisted up

---

25 I owe this insight to Dr. Mark Talbot.

on the tree, it endures pitiless scourging, so brutal that it brings him close to death's door. His throat is parched, his head bloodied by the thorns, his spirit utterly dejected by the mockery of the people that he had come to save. He screams from the cross, "God, why have you abandoned me?" The most important aspect of this cry of desolation is not, as some have imagined, that Jesus is bemoaning the weight of the Father's wrath now aimed at him instead of at the sinful world that he's saving. No, it's that in that wail, Christ expresses utter compassion toward the sufferer. To say that Christ suffered death and was buried is to claim that those who suffer are at the epicenter of God's empathy. God cares infinitely about the downtrodden. It is to say that *all* speaking of God must happen not only in the shadow of the cross, but *on the cross next to Christ.* In fact, before you even begin to speak *of* God, just start with the plea of the battered bandit: "Jesus, remember me."

To say that I felt abandoned by God in the hospital would be to assume that I was sensitive to the apparent departure of God's presence. In reality, I was far too numb by then to even realize the difference. I might have prayed once or twice, I forget. It's not really important. I didn't think God cared about me because God seemed perfectly content to perpetuate my time in that sorry place, allowing the initial suffering upon admission to compound itself into the most painful time I have ever known. But what if God was less concerned about the fact that I was suffering as with my belief that I was suffering alone? While I was in the hospital, I didn't think much about the suffering of Christ. Now I return again and again to that cryptic line of Paul's in which he claims that he is filling up the sufferings of Christ to their full measure. Was that what was happening in that ward? Is it even remotely possible that the suffering Christ was in me, *that Christ was suffering in me?* Perhaps.

Even now, time after time again, my flimsy power to believe in God seems utterly exhausted. Now as well. I ask: if I said something in the direction of heaven, would God actually hear it? To be honest, I haven't believed that for the last month or so. The heavens seem bolted shut, sealed off. Shout though I may, I am stuck in immanence, and God is beyond. I cannot reach beyond the fence of my own mind to grasp God, because every time I try, I end up with a God of my own invention. And as I look at my belief in God in years past, the prophecies of those postmodern seers— Marx, Feuerbach, Nietzsche—seem all to be accomplished in my own faith. Have I not believed in God because that belief perpetuated the privilege that sustained my comfort? Have I not created a deity in my own image, amplified his nature to the hundredth power, and ultimately proclaimed the fiction of my own mind the God of eternity? Have I not believed in God just so that I had something, anything to wield against those whom I resented: classmates, the native people of the country in which I will forever be a foreigner, anyone with whom I disagree? I don't think it's right to pray for the perpetuation of the systems that remove one from the misery of the grand majority of people on this earth. But now, I dare not pray at all for fear of imagining a God of my own making. Whether or not God has actually forsaken me is far beyond my knowledge, but I sure *feel* abandoned by God. And my only hope is that Christ, too, felt abandoned by the God whose peace and goodwill he had proclaimed all his life.

A Strange Abundance

For the Lord himself, with a cry of command,
with the archangel's call and with the sound
of God's trumpet, will descend from heaven,
and the dead in Christ will rise first.[26]

I had known Katrina distantly for a couple years. I remembered playing mandolin to her piano in an impromptu jam session three years ago and meeting again to play music a little while later. She was very complimentary during those times, and it was pretty clear that her effusive praise came out of insecurity more than anything else. One of the easiest things to do when you feel dismayed is to focus your attention on someone—anyone—who seems, unlike you, to have it together, and who might provide you with the attention and inspiration you need to pull through your present darkness. This, as I now know from both first- and third-person experience, is a cry for help veiled behind the sort of scrutiny and compliments that would make most people uncomfortable. Now as I look back on what Katrina once said of me, I imagine her grasping toward the hope that she desired and the fresh life that she wanted. A year passed before I saw her again, and when we met up, I had been slipping into depression.

This time, Katrina's gaze was steady. As she looked me in the eye without wavering, she told me how much she had changed. Yes, she had gone through a deep depression, but now she was well medicated and had found new hope. She was gainfully employed and was running triathlons *because she wanted to, because she could.* It was as if a switch had been flipped: the shallow plenteousness of her earlier words had given way to a new sincerity and a seemingly inexhaustible joy that now radiated outward from her. "I'm sorry that you're depressed," she said. "Don't ever give up on treatment; you never know what's right around the corner. I've been so different since doc put me on a new drug; just keep trying."

Katrina found me wavering on the verge of desperation. As I slipped into a depression, her words reminded me of that surreal joy that is often part of coming out of one. I've experienced it several times now. For months on end, the earth appears dull and gray, work seems (and often is) fruitless, the nights are shortened by insomnia and the days are harried by anxiety. Everything is slowed, and the darkness seems endless. And yet, as the grayscale of the world slowly shifts toward sepia and then to full color, where there once was despondency, a new wonder is born. This wonder, at least as I've experienced it, is not celestial or otherworldly. It is simply a return to what is, a seeing the truth of the world with eyes disabused of their dimness. As these renewed eyes revel in the bounty of a world that had long been hidden in darkness, a powerful question emerges: why? Why should I even be alive at all? Why does this scarred world still have such compelling beauty in it, the type of beauty that deserves to be laughed at or cried at or both? Why is it even remotely possible that the God who has seemed absent all this time actually exists? Why would anyone who has seen me during that harrowing darkness still love me, and why am I even allowed to experience the love of others when I have spent the last while despising myself? Now why shouldn't I do something extraordinary to celebrate this joy…like run a triathlon?

This wonder is the unexpected joy of the unexpected. The grim logic of suffering and death which dominates this world is completely coherent: children are born in poverty and die in misery, the best-laid plans crumble, power is sadism, and God is killed on the cross. But wonder—which is oftentimes a mere glimpse of joy—is made of a different stuff. It is apocalyptic, which means to say that it comes from beyond the horizons of our understanding and upsets them. Before it is ever an assertion of what is true (as in a theology of glory), it is a pressing query that calls the total reign of suffering into question. The wildflower in bloom, the patch of azure blue between the clouds, the unabashed grin of a friend each take their place on the witness stand and boldly claim that the logic of death does not yet have total control over the earth, that hope is real, that the thing we call life is actually well worth living, and that those isolated instances of hope and beauty are worth the ninety-nine moments of abjection in between them. They will not be silenced, for the joy that they proclaim is within their being and cannot stop overflowing the bounds of that being. Christ will not be laid in the tomb again.

The paradox of this post-depression wonder, and indeed wonder in general, is that it is both absolutely compelling and ephemeral. When it is there, it is so real. Unexpectedly, the world seems to burst forth toward me, and a satisfying bliss comes at the oddest of moments. But this beautiful wonder is like a wisp of smoke; I cannot seize it and grasp it for later. It is like the bread of heaven that would not be stored for more than a day before rotting, yet I cannot depend on it. I wish I could grasp it, but I cannot. Just as the dark mist of depression rises unexpectedly to give way to the bright rays of wonder, so too this wonder will slowly fade into the dark again. I cannot control wonder; it will not be contained. Just as the resurrected Christ would not allow the jubilant Mary Magdalene to cling to his side, so too the resurrection of joy to my soul will not be grasped onto. Just as the children in *The Chronicles of Narnia* could never count on Aslan to appear before them at any particular moment, so too I cannot count on the appearance of wonder. It will come and go just as freely and just as mysteriously as that mythical lion. But this too has reassurance in it, for since I cannot conjure up the joy of wonder, it will come without my willing it.

Katrina was right; you never know what's just around the corner. One of the most comforting thoughts while deep in depression is that just around the corner could be a new vista of joy.

Awaiting Fire

For who hopes for what is seen?[27]

Once I thought that God was speaking directly to me, his voice woven into the fabric of my thoughts. I no longer believe this, and the question of how I can hear the voice of God presents itself to me as urgently as ever. In a world filled with score upon score of would-be prophets, more or less honorable messengers of the divine, I yearn to *know* God. I thirst for just one instant in which the fog of my battered mind and the shroud of my human ignorance might be lifted such that I might know the God who *is*, not the God I presently imagine, whose nature shifts and bends with the whims of my mind. My thirst to hear the voice of God will not be quenched, and though I try to tamp it down, ignore it, and stifle it with a thousand distractions, it will not abate.

The fact that I haven't been able to disabuse myself of this longing is quite significant because I have indeed become very proficient at diverting myself from it. Silence is a sporadic and piecemeal part of my existence that I try to avoid as much as possible. No—I fight silence like the

---

27   Romans 8:24

plague. While biking to work, I always have music playing; the same music often accompanies me when I cook, clean, and walk. For significant stretches of time, I have almost managed to keep myself from praying entirely, because then I would have to acknowledge the silence that wraps itself around me, the silence that is the terrifying quiet of God. Likewise, I try tirelessly to avoid the sensation of solitude. When I am alone I keep myself occupied, preferably with something that will engross me to the point that I will, for the most part, be completely oblivious to the fact that I am in isolation. I reject any notion that God is using any particular experience to tell me something—as though the will of God for my life were understandable in the language and logic of my finite existence—outright. Just as someone who is tired of Lent, I groan under the weight of all those pieces of my life which remind me that I am mortal, that I know very little of the truth, and that my desires are muddled at best, depraved at worst.

No, my longing to hear the voice of God will not die. And even though I have learned the hard way not to trust the thousand impostors that present themselves as divine words in my mind and clamor for attention, I now acknowledge again the possibility that God is speaking to me inexplicably through the humdrum of every day. For to have faith is to believe that the impossible could actualize itself before your very eyes this moment, even if it never has and even if it never actually will. To believe in God is to believe in a spiritual world that is often beyond the bounds of your comprehension, that has the capacity to invade your narrow earthly existence and disrupt its all-too-human logic of rationalism and zero-sum games. Incidentally, faith in the impossible is something that can be livened by the surge and flow of mental illness. From time to time, an unthinkable terror comes upon me that is utterly beyond my capacity to understand, let alone to deal with. And likewise, just as I described in the previous chapter, the wonder that sometimes accompanies an exodus from depression is a similar vista onto the impossible actuality of life where there once was death. Though the possibility of God speaking to me in a way that I could understand seems remote, it could happen and perhaps it already is happening. The pain, the struggle, is to hold in tension God's silence and the possibility of hearing his voice.

In a sense, I feel my longing mirrors that of the early disciples before the Holy Spirit was sent on them. But it's different, because theirs was another sort of waiting for the voice of God. They had seen Christ appear to them and ascend into the heavens before their very eyes, and they waited in the assurance that the upstart Galilean rabbi that they had walked with for those three long years was in fact the master of death and of the momentary silence in which they lived. I suspect this is why Luke hardly skips a beat between the moments that Christ ascends and the Spirit descends, because this assurance makes the waiting seem insubstantial. Faith is a spectrum from assurance to doubt (because indifference is more truly the opposite of faith than skepticism), and the post-resurrection faith of the apostles was extremely on the side of assurance. The trajectory of their lives—from belief in Christ to the mandate to go to the ends of the earth—had already been set; to their very deaths they fed off of the momentum of the resurrection. And while I try to follow in the footsteps of the apostles' teaching, their unshakeable faith seems foreign to me. To be sure, I live by the same faith and hope in Christ that they did, but while they express their faith in an unshakeable certainty that led many of them to martyrdom, my faith often seems to be just stable enough to keep me alive for another month. And while they awaited the coming of the Holy Ghost with a victorious assurance, I wonder if one day God will speak to me as he did to them. At the end of the day, I can identify more with Israel in the centuries directly before the coming of Christ—enemies on every side and a dearth of divine words—than with the apostles as they awaited the coming of the Holy Spirit. Even so, I believe that my faith will also endure to my death, because if I lose faith, by what else can I live? And where there is faith, there is waiting, a wizened hope in the not-yet.

Meaning and the Body

For no one ever hates his own body.[28]

It is a month before my wedding, and I'm wondering whether my existence is worthwhile at all. Fortunately, I'm not alone, but in the company of my fiancée Laurie. Like Whac-A-Moles that pop up incessantly on their arcade landscape, the same questions recur incessantly in our conversation: "Do you love me?" "Do you want me around?" "Do I suck?" When I ask her these things, I recognize, however dimly, that my depression is causing me to have a skewed view of reality—particularly of my own value—and that I need Laurie to remind me of the truths that do not ebb or flow with my moods. And she does. She is kind and patient, and sometimes when I look her in the eyes I weep to see how well she loves me.

I don't have much advice to offer to people who have a desperate depression or rabid anxiety, mainly because I think their state should evoke words of compassion, not suggestions on how to deal with it. But here is one piece of advice: seek out loved ones who want to be with you when you are at the end of your rope. To be depressed is

28 Ephesians 5:29

to be isolated, for the symptoms of depression—inexplicable sadness, numbness, shame, and hopelessness, just to name a few—serve to rend you from the social space in which woes are experienced, understood, and shouldered communally. If you are deeply depressed, even the smallest move toward community is arduous, for it runs against the grain of the isolation inherent to your mental state. To make the call to a friend, assuming the weight of your perceived worthlessness on staggering limbs, requires the strength of Atlas; to answer the question "how are you?" candidly and confidently requires the power of Hercules. But those who are willing to experience your misery and even your desperation with you perpetually work against the isolation of depression. Their words and glances interrogate that gnawing, melancholy stillness, and make you wonder if your despondency will have the last word after all. Slowly, the presence of friends erodes the mass of confusion and self-hatred and gradually strengthens your eyes to look at your state with their gentleness and impartiality. And if you learn from their tenacious love, you will discover much about where significance lies.

By the logic of this world, value is utility, and the differentiation of the value of two people is a matter of discerning their marginal utilities. In this immanent calculus, a human goal is postulated, and individuals are weighed in the balance by their capacity to bring this goal about. Only the fittest survive, and those unfortunate ones who have been deemed insufficient must resign themselves to the careers of bottom-dwellers. Within this system, charity is inefficiency, for to spend a moment attending to the sorrows of another is to temporarily set aside one's aspirations of grandeur and perhaps thereby forfeit them. This paradigm—the paradigm of utility—is so deeply ingrained within us that most of us do not even notice the ways in which we silently evaluate everyone around us by their power, wisdom, capital, and suitability to our desires. Of course, we turn this calculus on ourselves too, and when we do this there is no happy medium—either we are lost in delusions of our own supremacy or staggered by our own futility. And futility is unavoidable, for if we shrink a person to a mere object and evaluate him for his utility, we will always find him wanting.

But our very marrow cries out against this reductionist calculus that will make the most wonderful of all of God's creations—a human being—a mere cog in a machine. Every pair of eyes that our eyes meet speaks their meaning to us and reflects our own meaning back to us. The truth of existence, not some artificial understanding of utility, is the measure of meaning, for our value is intrinsic, not extrinsic. It is not afforded to us by some miserly mill owner who, at the end of the day, gives our weary hands meaning in the form of two copper coins to rub together. No, it is given to our unseeing hands that clutch and grasp at the air as they emerge from the womb. Of course, it is a gift far too weighty for human hands; neither infant hands nor the most mature fingers can contain the significance that is fearfully endowed to humans. All too often, it will burst beyond the grip of our fleshly hands and shoot upwards, taking our gaze with it. The good news—creation, incarnation, resurrection—is the truth that human beings, corrupt and mortal though they are, have a wonderfully important part to play in the restoration of all things. Their participation in this celestial drama is not contingent on application or interview; it is given to them in the form of their faltering human flesh. If it is true that God is redeeming the world, then we don't need to be particularly holy or special to participate in that redemption. We do not need to fight for his consideration as the world fights; our mere existence is assurance enough that God's summing up of all that is in Christ will not exclude us.

We learn of meaning in communities of inclusion. The world includes selectively on the basis of marginal utility and pedigree, which is to say that it excludes. The exclusion of the world is never for good reason. For to exclude based on race, gender, sex, or capital assumes that the value of a human being is found in their participation in a group (oftentimes a group they could not even choose), whereas in reality, the value of a human being precedes their inclusion in any worldly group. The value of humans is not a hierarchy; it is an axiom. Try as we may—and have we tried!—we cannot do anything to efface the reality of a single person. It is within inclusive communities (ideally: the church) that we come to understand that our meaning is not a matter of contingencies, but is affixed to us. Within these communities, the generous logic of love can triumph over the withholding logic of utility.

When I think of the power of inclusion, I remember my friend Iliana Rivera. Iliana has suffered from myasthenia gravis since she was thirteen. She needs a scooter to get around, and work is extraordinarily hard for her body, which is engaged in a lifelong fight against itself. Victories do not come easy to Iliana: she started owning her faith as a teenager while imploring God to let her smile again, she graduated from college by taking frequent all-nighters because her body was often too tired to work during the day, and she finally received much-needed disability income after years of trying to convince the Illinois courts that her condition makes holding a job challenging at best. Not only does Iliana face the physical hardship of her illness, but every day she must contend with our society's everyday condescension toward the disabled. Motorists stare at her, some professors reject her requests to waive or change her assignments so that she can complete them, some staff members are unwilling to adjust a largely inaccessible campus to accommodate her, and everybody seems to think that she'd be better off if she didn't aspire to achievements that are best left for able people. Why is it only Iliana's friends who get to see something of her incredible strength? For Iliana is not only an unyielding advocate for those with disabilities, but an avid participant in the struggle for racial and gender equality. Watching Iliana's patience with me—a white male who is still unknowingly racist and sexist in so many ways—has taught me much. Not least, it has taught me that sometimes I need to do my own research and give people of color a break from the questions about race that they are often bombarded with. Iliana is a living testament to the truth that the value of a human being is not derived from her utility, but from her being.

I have to believe in the intrinsic value of human life, for otherwise my own life would have no meaning. For all intents and purposes, I am mostly useless right now. It is all that I can do to hold down a small part-time job and cook and clean with Laurie; beyond that, I do very little that is useful. From time to time, I'll share coffee with a friend, and perhaps they might leave the better for it. I am a liability to most employers—who wants to hire someone who got let go from his last job for mental illness? If there truly is no meaning to be found beyond driving the economy, succeeding in the eyes of friends, and reaching the highest status possible, then I am lost—or perhaps, in the words of St. Paul, "of all people most to be pitied." And sometimes it seems that this is so. But then I look someone whom I love in the eye and realize that it is not.

The Good Fight

The Lord will take his zeal as his whole armor.[29]

I once heard a scholar suggest that the allied invasion of Normandy succeeded because the troops that arrived on the beach knew that there was no going back. Where could they flee? Behind them was only the hard metal of the landing craft, half-decimated already by the bullets of the machine guns, and the cold surf of the English Channel. Storming the beach was likely death, but attempting to swim the English Channel back to the relative safety of war-torn England was certain death. They had nowhere to go but forward.

The thought of those brave soldiers—or at least, soldiers forced into bravery—has stuck with me and reminds me of the odd things that can happen to one whose back is against the wall. For in those situations, a remarkable pragmatism can take control, the pragmatism that weighs the impossible against the inconceivable and chooses between them. The soldiers knew that they could not return to England, but the task before them—navigating hundreds of yards of iron barbs, dead bodies, bloodied sand, and hellish horror—was simply unfathomable. Seeing the dilemma before them, their resolve was strengthened and their bravery immortalized. To say that they chose the hard path is not exactly true, for they chose the *only* path, the only option in a dearth of alternatives. They chose to fight; choosing to do what otherwise was impossible. Sometimes I imagine myself in their shoes, for though my situation is vastly different than theirs, I am often faced with a similar choice when my back is up against the wall. My junior year, when I realized that the God who had told me that I was going to marry someone who had no interest in me was a sham of my own creation. My senior year, when hour after miserable hour in the hospital dragged by and my thoughts flew toward destruction. The summer after graduation, when I realized that the only thing keeping me from marrying Laurie was the fear that I wouldn't be able to be a good husband to her, even though she had often assured me that she would take care of me and that she thought I *would* be a good husband. The choices I made in those times and indeed still make every day are respectively the existential decisions for faith, life, and love. These are the things that I am called to.

I use "called to" intentionally: vocation consists not of a career, but of a life. We imagine sometimes that one's calling is a matter of a job; while jobs are of utmost importance, to reduce the language of vocation to occupation is to shrivel it. When Paul speaks of the irrevocable calling of God, he means a calling to participate in the divine life, to be *in* the death and resurrection of Christ, to have faith, hold on to hope, love. To be sure, vocation is not a matter of abstractions; one is called to particular people and to particular things. The things that you are called to are the stuff of your life, to lose them is the greatest loss and to forsake them is

to die a real death long before your breath stops and your
eyes freeze in their place.

Oddly enough, the things that we are called to are
always problematic. We have long left that land of ideals
that was the garden of Eden. Now every reality we commit
ourselves to is a sorry replica of that pre-fall perfection and
will, at some point, frustrate even the most meticulous of
our attempts to attend to it. To be part of a church is to
immerse oneself in the sufferings and imperfections of not
just one other follower of Christ—but scores of them. To
learn to make a musical instrument sing as naturally as
your own voice is to be brought up short again and again
by your ineptitude, and then by your lack of patience. Try
as we may, we will find no thing that will not frustrate our
attention, no person that will not at some time dishearten
us if we heed them for long. Even in the most ideal of
circumstances, existence is a struggle. The act of love and
the satisfaction in the things that we love will not always
come easily to us, and when they do not, then is the time
to fight, to fight for love itself. The fight begins with the
simple truth that there is no other alternative to fighting.

If the good fight begins with desperation, it is sustained
with anger. Anger is highly stigmatized in western society;
I imagine this is in part because many of the unjust systems
that we've erected depend on not too many people's getting
angry at the injustice that they perpetuate. Anger ought not
be stigmatized, for it is an extremely important part of a
healthy emotional life. It is an adversarial emotion which
empowers against-ness. Genuine anger is not equivalent
to hatred, for it arises when the attention of love finds an
object that is unjust and contrary to flourishing. Genuine
anger is not rage, for while rage thwarts all means of con-

trolling it, anger can indeed be channeled into actions that counteract the thing it opposes. If it were not for anger, we would have no independence struggles, no civil rights marches, no resistance to the thousand ways in which the rulers, powers, and authorities of the present day clasp the inhabitants of the earth in bondage and make them eat the dust of which they are made. *If Christ was not angry at the stranglehold of sin and the domination of the oppressed, he would never have gone to the cross*, nor risen from the tomb in victory over death. To participate in Christ is, not least, to participate in his anger recounted in the Gospels, his anger for the sake of the world.

The logic of anger within depression is confounding. If I am able to parse out the elements of my depression (which I cannot always do, for depression makes me feel extremely numb), I often find that I am silently livid at myself for being depressed. When I do this, I take one of my most powerful emotions and turn it against myself. Little wonder that depression makes me extremely weary, for the weight of my own anger is staggering. Just like anxiety, the anger of depression has to be channeled for it to be healthy. First, it must be turned outwards. Guilt is the only right occasion for being angry at oneself, and while being depressed often causes the perception of guilt, it never renders one guilty of anything. Secondly, the anger must be put in the service of working against its rightful object. If this object is the depression itself, then the anger might be used to do some of the most difficult things to do when depressed—reaching out for help, taking part in something gratuitously enjoyable, describing one's emotional state to another person. Slowly, the anger of helplessness can give way to the anger of empowerment. As I push anger outwards, it pulls me toward a desperate world, a world that needs someone to be angry for its sake. In particular, it leads me to do everything that I can possibly do to advocate for those who cannot stand up to advocate for themselves. Theirs is truly the good fight; theirs is the kingdom of heaven.

Tears in Heaven

Would you know my name if I saw you in heaven?[30]

From time to time, I yearn for the kingdom yet to come. But then the questions catch up to me, and I'm lost.

If scripture in general raises more questions than it answers, the same is true in the extreme for the book of Revelation. The book produces a similar effect to the heavy use of incense at a high church: its metaphors and symbolism overload the senses and obscure everything in a cloud of mystery. Is it possible to take *anything* in the book of Revelation literally? And if the contents of the book are only to be understood metaphorically, what do they mean? The exhortations in Revelation—to hold on to hope and persevere through all types of earthly tribulation—are clear, but the contents of that hope are not. What is the pearly-gated city that will descend to earth at the end of the age? How will we like it there, accustomed as we are to our worldly existence? Will we be able to stomach the coming kingdom, or will its very grass puncture our feeble feet as we tread on it, as in Lewis' *The Great Divorce*? And these questions, compelling though they are, only concern

---

30 Eric Clapton, "Tears in Heaven"

the human race considered in its entirety. What about the particulars of our persons? How will they translate into the coming kingdom?

Will my mind be so transformed that I am never depressed again? If so, what will my mind be like? Will I be eternally hypomanic, forever visited by the same state that has given the world so many of its greatest works of art? Will my mind finally be stable, and, if so, will it forever be blissful? Most Christians assume that the eschaton will be perpetual bliss for all who are called to it, but this notion seems really problematic. An existence in which we are perpetually and inescapably happy seems a fate more like that of Homer's lotus eaters than that of a truly redeemed human being. I don't desire to live in a world in which I constantly experience the height of ecstasy, for such a world fails to fulfill. On earth, happiness is a transient emotional state that actually prevents flourishing if it is perpetuated too long. Is it even hypothetically possible that an overabundance of happiness could tend toward the fullness of life that Christ promises? Can we be truly happy if we do not cry?

This last question is particularly captivating to me because crying over suffering is one of the most healing things I can do. For in that act, I validate the pain that has been felt and surrender to its truth, allowing its implications to shape me and move me. Through crying, I express sorrow to those around me in a compelling, sublinguistic way that many humans find deeply compelling and meaningful. Crying is truth-telling and meaning-making and remembrance, for in crying you convey the truth of the past and allow that truth to reach you in the present, giving into its import, acknowledging its meaning. How are we supposed to worship the lamb who was slain with dry eyes? Do we expect that whenever we are moved by his suffering, the Father will come and comfort us with a simple "there, there, it's all right now, there are no tears here"? To attempt to speak of divine truth in general and the coming kingdom in particular requires a great deal of humility and a perpetual willingness to be wrong, and I can only imagine how silly and insignificant these questions which seem so pressing now will prove to be upon the return of Christ. But I ask them with such urgency now because they point to a great mystery of the world to come, a mystery into which I long to peer until I am blinded by the sight.

My worldly eyes are indeed quickly blinded by those glimpses of that coming kingdom. I can tell this by how very slow I am to recognize all the ways in which humans are unjust. Many of these ways are perniciously subtle, lying far below the gaze of our oblivious eyes. If you had tried to talk to me a mere five years ago about commonplace racial profiling, I would not have understood. Nor would I have understood if you explained the current environmental crises, the connection between consumer goods and the oppression of the poor in non-western countries, our obliviousness to animal suffering, our disregard for the homeless, and mass incarceration. To be sure, I might have been able to conceptually grasp the importance and even the tragedy of all these phenomena, but by no means would I have realized my own implication in them in the everyday choices that I make, let alone begun to change those behaviors which contribute to injustice. To be unaware of one's own involvement in relationships of oppression is to be blind to the coming kingdom, for its ruler is the prince of *shalom* whose very resurrection is the triumph of the oppressed. Inasmuch as we are presently blind to injustice, we are also unseeing of the kingdom of justice. In large part, we can tell how quickly we will adjust to the new heavens and the new earth by our readiness to change our unjust behaviors. If we cannot imagine taking concrete steps to living in peace with our neighbor now, we cannot begin to imagine the kingdom to come.

The book of Revelation was not written for those who already live in the new heavens and the new earth, but for those who await them. It is not written to those whose eyes no longer cry (if that passage is to be taken literally), but to those whose eyes are now full of tears and often find themselves baptized by a seemingly unending sorrow. The purpose of John's revelation is not to provide disciples with a systematic account of the kingdom to come but to steel their wavering resolve for the patch of road immediately ahead of them. There is no need for sugarcoating the realities of our existence in this present age: even a few steps on the road to the redemption of all things can be brutal. But I've realized over the last months that to continue along the fraught path of existence is to hope. It seems not a day goes by without the thought of suicide occurring to me. The majority of the time, it is merely a passing specter that flies past my mind as quickly as it came. But sometimes that thought, like a bird, alights in my mind and makes its sorry nest there for a matter of moments. In those moments I feel as small, worthless, and insignificant as a gnat in a ditch. It is there that I remember, though I work constantly and desperately toward fullness of life, that I do not know how much longer I will have to struggle until the resurrection of the dead. I do not know the fate of the house in Oregon I now call home, much less the future of the fragile globe that we live on. I am often overwhelmed by the many things outside of my control and fear that my hard-earned breath will be whisked away by violence or chance. But I know that to hope is to keep believing that God is redeeming the world, even now, and that somehow my existence and communion with the beloved people who surround me are truly important to that redemption. And to hope is not only to believe that, but to act on it. For me, acting on the hope of renewal is oftentimes as basic as deciding to continue living for one more week. As I make this choice for life again and again, these two truths comprehend all meaning for me:

I am not alone, and walking the road of hope is always worth it.

Made in the USA
Columbia, SC
21 September 2018